Gladys Evelyne Wright
911 Garfield Ave
Marietta, Ohio

.70

ROMA

CAMBRIDGE
UNIVERSITY PRESS
LONDON: BENTLEY HOUSE
NEW YORK, TORONTO, BOMBAY
CALCUTTA, MADRAS: MACMILLAN

Photo Alinari

SLOPES OF THE CAPITOL SEEN FROM THE FORUM

ROMA

A READER FOR THE SECOND STAGE OF LATIN

by

C. E. ROBINSON

Assistant Master at Winchester College

and

P. G. HUNTER

Assistant Master at Stowe School

CAMBRIDGE

AT THE UNIVERSITY PRESS

1942

By C. E. Robinson

LATINUM

First stage: Translations etc. for beginners

ROMANI

Third stage: Suitable for pre-certificate year

First Edition 1938
Reprinted 1942

PRINTED IN GREAT BRITAIN

PREFACE

The main purpose of this book is to introduce young students to the work of Latin authors and the main outline of Roman History at the earliest possible stage. The Latin itself has of necessity undergone some modification and simplification; but it has been our aim to retain in a large degree the flavour of the original. The extracts, chosen in the first place for their intrinsic interest, serve also to illustrate the more important phases of Republican and Imperial History, as set forth in the historical sketch.

Special attention has been paid to the building up of a vocabulary which will form a sound foundation for further reading: and the choice of words for memorisation is largely based on the selection made by Professor G. Lodge of Columbia University and bearing a strict relation to the frequency of their use in the best Latin authors.

The book is intended, as its title suggests, to introduce the student to the use of *compound* sentences, involving participles, temporal clauses, final clauses, and simple indirect speech. The order in which these appear has been carefully graduated; and the exercises for retranslation (which are related to the Latin pieces in vocabulary and content) correspond under the following scheme:

I–V.	Relatives.
VI–XIII *b*.	Participles (Ablative Absolute).
XIV *a*–XVII.	Indirect Statements.
XVIII–XXIV.	Mixed Participles.
XXV–XXVI *b*.	Revision: the use of cases.
XXVII–XXIX.	Final Clauses.
XXX–XXXII.	Indirect Commands.
XXXIII–XXXV.	Finals and Indirect Commands.
XXXVI–XXXVIII.	Indirect Questions.

From piece XXXIX onwards there is a reversion to a simpler level of style; and the remainder of the book may well be used for purposes of revision. The exercises accompanying these later pieces are of a varying nature; but a further selection of sentences for revision will be found near the end of the book, and sentences could be made up for the same purpose as follows:

XXXIX *a*, *b*.	Relatives.
XXXIX *c*, XLIV.	Ablative Absolute.
XXXIX *d*, XLI *b*.	Deponent Participles.
XL *a*, XLVI.	Indirect Statements.
XL *b*.	Finals and Indirect Commands.
XLII, XLV.	Mixed Participles.
XLIII, LVI.	Cases.
XLIX *a*.	Indirect Questions.
L *a*, *b*, LI.	Indirect Statements, Commands and Questions.
LV.	Indirect Statements and Commands.

Concerning the Vocabularies, certain points should be noted:

(1) The Special Vocabularies, accompanying each piece, are intended for strict memorisation.

(2) Vocabulary I, at the end of the book, contains words with which, it is assumed, the student will already be familiar.

(3) In Vocabulary II words which have previously occurred in the Special Vocabularies are accompanied by a mere reference back to the Special Vocabulary in which they occurred.

In the Latin selections, the quantities of long vowels have been marked where it has seemed desirable: fully down to and including Exercise XXIV, subsequently only to a small extent.

C. E. R.
P. G. H.

30 *July* 1938

HISTORICAL OUTLINE

[*The Roman numerals refer to the Latin pieces chosen to illustrate Roman history.*]

Our own history begins with legends—of King Arthur and his knights. Roman history began with legends too. When Troy (they said) was besieged and captured by the Greeks (I, II), a Trojan warrior, Aeneas, escaped and sailed to Italy (III). There his descendants settled in Alba, the 'White City'; and it was by one of these, Romulus, that Rome was eventually founded in 753 B.C. (IV, V, VI). Under the succeeding line of kings the tiny state flourished, until Tarquin the Proud by his tyrannous rule enraged the citizens and was expelled in 510 B.C. The neighbouring Etruscans tried to restore him but were beaten back (VII, VIII); and henceforward for nearly five centuries Rome remained a Republic. She was governed by two *consuls*, annually elected and assisted by a permanent council or *senate*.

At first there were serious class conflicts. The Patricians or 'gentry' bullied the Plebeians or 'commoners', allowing them no share in the government. One day, in 494 B.C., the Plebeians in exasperation marched out of the city and refused to return until they were granted the right of electing champions of their own, called *tribunes* (IX*a* and *b*). Little by little the masses gained more say in affairs; and, when in 450 B.C. a certain Appius Claudius tried to abuse his official power, he was foiled by their stout resistance (X).

The Romans were, in fact, great lovers of liberty; but they loved discipline even more. Throughout their history they were famous for their patriotism and for their military prowess. Their army was composed of ordinary citizens, called up (when need arose) from plough or workshop. Even a leading general might have to be fetched from his farm at a crisis (XI). Wars were frequent against the Volscians and other surrounding tribes (XII). But by the start of the fourth century B.C. Rome had begun to gain the upper hand.

Then suddenly in 390 B.C. came a terrible catastrophe. A barbarian horde of Gauls, crossing the Alps, marched south and sacked the city (XIII *a* and *b*). Happily they soon departed; and with amazing pluck the little Republic recovered. In bitter wars (327–290) she overcame the Samnites and the remaining Italian tribes (XIV *a* and *b*). Finally came a conflict with the cities founded by Greek colonists in the south. These called to their aid a Greek prince, Pyrrhus (XV); and his well-trained army was almost too much for the Romans. But their tenacity triumphed, and by 270 B.C. they were masters of the whole Italian peninsula.

Across the Mediterranean on the African coast lay a great rival, Carthage. Her wealthy merchants kept a strong fleet and hired mercenary troops. Most of Sicily was under their control; and here Rome challenged them (264–241), building for the first time a fleet of her own and even sending an expedition to Africa itself (XVI, XVII). This expedition failed, but after twenty years of war Sicily was wrested from Carthage.

A generation later a young Carthaginian general, Hannibal, determined on revenge. Starting from Spain (much of which his father had conquered), he marched his army across the Alps and in 218 descended upon Italy. At Lake Trasimene and elsewhere he inflicted terrible defeats on the Romans (XVIII, XIX). But he could not take the city (XX). His brother Hasdrubal, bringing reinforcements from Spain, was destroyed (XXI); and after fourteen years spent on Italian soil, Hannibal was forced to return to Africa, there to be defeated by Scipio at Zama in 202. Some years later he died an exile in a foreign land (XXII).

At Rome meanwhile Scipio was the hero of the hour. Opponents tried to discredit him, but failed miserably (XXIII). He was a rare spirit; and, unlike most of his ignorant and superstitious fellow-countrymen (XXIV), he loved learning. He and his friends greatly admired the quick-witted Greeks and studied their wonderful literature. When in 196, after fighting a successful war against Philip, King of Macedon, they might have annexed Greece, they preferred to proclaim all her cities free from Philip's sway (XXV).

Not all Romans were so generous-minded. Many feared that Greek learning would make men soft. Cato, in particular, maintained that the country was 'going to the dogs' and strove to restore the strict habits of 'the good old days' (XXVI *a* and *b*). He considered that Roman interests should at all costs come first. During a visit to Carthage he witnessed signs of her returning prosperity; and 'Carthage must be destroyed' became henceforth his slogan. A quarrel was picked: and in 146 after a terrible siege the proud city was razed to the ground (XXVII). About the same time Rome also annexed Macedon and completed the conquest of Spain. By 135 B.C. her empire embraced all the western half of the Mediterranean basin. Even the monarchs of the eastern half, though still unconquered, acknowledged her supremacy (XXVIII).

The Republic ruled its empire with a heavy hand. Of the governors, who were sent out to its new provinces, some strove to be severely just: many were grasping (L *a* and *b*); a few were treacherous and cruel (XXIX). At home the Senate's rule was becoming selfish and oppressive. A small group of noble families held all the power, making sure by bribery and similar means that their own members were elected to the consulship and other offices. Most Italian land, too, was taken up by the estates of these same nobles. Thousands of small farmers lost their acres and crowded into Rome as 'unemployed'. At last in 132 Tiberius Gracchus proposed that small allotments should be found for them; but the senatorial nobles opposed him and he was killed in a riot (xxx). His brother, Gaius Gracchus, took up the cause of the poor. He spoke out for the Italian peasantry who suffered from the overbearing behaviour of the nobles (xxxi); but he too was killed.

Gaius Gracchus had won the support of the middle-class business-men who resented the nobles' power; and these business-men now formed a party eager to discredit the Senate. Their chance soon came. A war broke out against Jugurtha, a nomad prince of Africa. The senatorial generals bungled it; and the people in exasperation sent out Gaius Marius, a man of the despised middle-class. He won the war and reorganised the army. It was well he did so. For at this moment came a terrible threat of invasion. A barbarian host of Cimbri and Teutoni marched down out of north Europe. Marius saved the day by meeting them in southern Gaul and defeating them utterly in 102 B.C. (xxxii).

Marius, with his victorious army at his back, had the chance of dominating the State. He made little use of it; and soon a Civil War (in which the Italians fought Rome and fought successfully to win the rights of citizenship) brought a rival general to the fore. This man, Sulla, threw his weight on the side of the Senate and against the middle-class faction; and Marius after a series of hair-breadth escapes was hunted out of Italy (xxxiii). While Sulla was absent on a foreign campaign, Marius returned and massacred many senators. Then Sulla came home eager for revenge and it was the turn of the middle-class to be massacred (xxxiv *a* and *b*). But, despite Sulla's attempt to restore it, the Senate's power was fast waning. It was incapable even of controlling the mob within the capital itself. In 63 Catiline attempted to raise a revolution; and his plot was barely foiled by the cool courage of Cicero (xxxvi).

Troubles were only beginning. Fresh wars brought forward fresh generals as competitors for power. First, Pompey was sent out against Mithridates, a native king of Asia Minor; and there he followed up his victory by annexing the whole Syrian coast and capturing the town of Jerusalem (XXXV). But on his return to Rome Pompey proved incapable of restoring order. Ambitious politicians hired bodyguards of ruffians and murderous brawls were frequent (XXXVII). Meanwhile another and greater leader was emerging—Gaius Julius Caesar, a man as brilliant and masterful as ever lived (XXXVIII). He first won his position by achieving the conquest of Gaul, 58–55 B.C. In 55 and 54 he invaded Britain (XXXIX *a*, *b*, *c*, *d*); he then spent some years in crushing a dangerous Gallic insurrection led by Vercingetorix (XL *a*, *b*). Finally, at the head of his victorious legions, he determined to make himself master of Rome. Pompey, now the Senate's champion, rallied their forces in Greece; but in 48 B.C. he was defeated near Pharsalia (XLI *b*). Caesar was now lord of the world; and under him Rome ceased to be a Republic. He did not actually abolish the Senate, but the nobles found his dictatorship so intolerable that in 44 B.C. they plotted to kill him (XLII).

Caesar's death brought on fresh civil wars, out of which, in 31 B.C., his young heir Augustus came victorious. More tactful than Caesar, he honoured the Senate and gave them a share of power. He restored peace and prosperity to the Empire (XLIII); but his attempt to conquer Germany ended in A.D. 9 in utter disaster (XLIV). He was followed by four Emperors all sprung from one branch or other of his family. Tiberius (A.D. 14–37) began well and ended badly. Caligula was mad. Claudius (A.D. 41–54) was ruled by his favourites. Nero (A.D. 54–68) abused his power so grossly that the armies came out in revolt; and he committed suicide (XLV).

There followed a fresh Civil War between rival generals. Victory went to Vespasian (A.D. 69–79), an Emperor of a new type, a man of the middle-class who reorganised the army and finance on business-like lines (XLVI). Under him the government of the Empire grew more systematic; and after the death of his son Domitian (XLVII) it became the custom to choose emperors by merit rather than by lineage. A brilliant era now began. The officials ruled the provinces with justice, referring all difficult problems to their master. We have a letter in which one of them asked the advice of Trajan (A.D. 98–117) about the treatment of Christians; and we have Trajan's reply (XLIX *a* and *b*). Law and order prevailed as never before; and Europe still owes much to the methods that such men devised for impartial and efficient administration.

Besides good government, the Empire gave Europe civilisation. The influence of Greek culture, we must remember, had transformed the Romans. They were no longer simple farmers like Cincinnatus of old. Their leaders were highly educated gentlemen. They produced great poets like Vergil, great historians like Livy. Magnificent temples and public halls were built. The provincials too were encouraged to build towns with imposing squares and amphitheatres and public baths. Education spread through Spain, Gaul and Britain (XLVIII). Under the Emperor Hadrian (A.D. 117–137)—himself a student and a poet (LXXV)—the height of the Empire's prosperity was reached. The following centuries witnessed a long decline. There were terrible civil wars. Food ran short; for it became impossible for the farmers to produce enough both for the luxurious town populations and for the armies which guarded the frontiers. There meanwhile fresh hordes of barbarians were pressing hard along the Rhine and the Danube. Eventually they broke through into the provinces of the West. Rome herself was sacked in A.D. 410; and her great Empire went to pieces. Only the Eastern half withstood the shock: and under the rule of the Byzantine Emperors its capital Constantinople survived for another thousand years.

CONTENTS

ILLUSTRATIONS

CONNECTION

In English a series of ideas is often expressed by a series of *simple* sentences. Thus: 'The horse fell. Alexander struck the coachman a blow. He was furiously angry.' A Latin writer's methods were somewhat different.

I. He was more careful to connect his sentences by conjunctions, thus showing whether a sentence stood to what preceded it as cause, or consequence, or whatever it might be.

Thus: 'Cecidit equus. Alexander *igitur* raedarium verberavit; *nam* magna ira commovebatur.' 'The horse fell. Alexander *therefore* struck the coachman; *for* he was moved by great anger.'

It is very important to recognise the significance of these conjunctions. Some (printed with dots following) come first word in the sentence. Others (printed with dots preceding) come later, usually second.

But. Sed ...; ... tamen; ... autem; verum ...; ... vero.
Therefore. Itaque ...; ... igitur; ergo....
For. Nam ...; ... enim.

Note also adverbs of time which often serve as links in narrative: *deinde*, *tum* (then); *interea* (meanwhile); *tandem*, *denique* (at length); *statim* (at once).

II. Very frequently the Latin writer would express a series of two (or more) ideas in a single *compound* sentence. In this one idea would be the main clause; the other would be subordinate, either (*a*) as a *participle*: e.g. Alexander, magna ira *commotus*, raedarium verberavit; or (*b*) as a *dependent* clause: e.g. *quod* (because) equus *cecidit*, magna ira commovebatur.

Often both methods would be combined: e.g. Alexander, quod equus cecidit, magna ira commotus, raedarium verberavit.

I. HELEN ELOPES WITH PARIS

This Greek legend was an attempt to explain the cause of the Trojan War.

Fuit ōlim in Asiā urbs magna, quae Trōja nōminābātur. Hūjus urbis rex Priamus fīliōs habuit multōs, quōrum ūnus, **nōmine** Paris, ad Graeciam **vēnit.** Ibi Menelāus, rex Spartōrum, eum hospitiō accēpit, fraudem nōn timens. Uxor vērō Menelāī fuit Helena, fēmina clārissima, quam **propter** pulchritūdinem omnēs Graecī laudābant. Hanc, ubi vīderat, Paris statim amāvit. **Consilium** igitur **cēpit audācissimum**, de quō multōs diēs silēbat. Tum mediā nocte Helenam clam rapuit; in nāvem cum eā ascendit; Trōjam trans mare **petiit.**

II. THE SIEGE OF TROY

After ten years of siege and the death of Hector the Trojan champion, the city was taken by the famous ruse of the wooden horse.

Raptā Helenā, concurrunt Graecī; rēgēs eōrum consilium capiunt; mille nāvēs parant, in quibus Trōjam trans mare petunt. Sīc **incēpit** bellum Trōjānum, dē quō scripsit Homērus, poētārum clārissimus. Decem annōs urbem obsident Graecī, dēfendunt Trōjānī. Deinde Achillēs, vir Graecōrum fortissimus, quem propter ferōcitātem Trōjānī timē-

nōmen, -inis (neut.), *name* — Eng. *nominal*
venio,[1] -ire, vēni, ventum, *come* — Fr. *venir*
propter (prep.), *on account of, because of*
consilium, -i (neut.), *plan, intention, advice*
capio,[2] -ere, cēpi, captum, *take, seize, capture*
audax (adj.), *bold, resolute, audacious*
peto, -ere, -īvi (-ii), -itum, *seek, ask, look for, make for* — Eng. *petition*

II

incipio, -ere, -cēpi, -ceptum, *begin, start*

[1] Note the compounds: *advenio* (*ad*), *pervenio* (*ad*), reach, arrive (at); *invenio*, find, discover; *circumvenio*, surround.

[2] Note the compounds: *accipio*, receive, accept; *recipio*, take back, receive; *incipio*, begin; *suscipio*, undertake.

bant, ad mūrōs ipsōs **prōgreditur**. Cuī obviam it Hector, Priamī rēgis **fīlius**; sed, **subitō** timōre captus, fugit; circum **mūrōs** ter currit; tandem hastā, quam alter magnā vī **jēcit**, transfīgitur et dēlapsus moritur.

III. THE FLIGHT OF AENEAS

The Romans, wishing to connect their own history with Greek legend, believed that Aeneas founded the race from which Rome eventually sprang.

Trōjā ā Graecis captā, Aenēās cum suīs fūgit. Fīlium suum **manū** tenēbat. Patrem suum, quī jam senex erat, umerīs **portābat**. Sequēbātur uxor ējus, cuī nōmen erat Creūsa; sed, nocte veniente, suōs vidēre nōn poterat et ē viā errāvit. Aenēās, ad **portam** urbis veniens, uxōrem **quaerere** incipit; nōmine eam appellat; sed respondet nēmo. Patre et fīliō **relictīs**, in urbem redit; viam vīcīnōsque locōs explōrat; sed eam invenīre nōn potest. Tum, uxōre perditā, ad mare abit et in nāvem, quam **parāverat**, cum suīs ascendit. Post multōs annōs ad Ītaliam pervenit.

prōgredior,[1] -i, -gressus, *go forward, advance, proceed* — Eng. *progress*
fīlius, -i (masc.), *son* — Fr. *fils*
subitus (adj.), *sudden, unexpected.* (Adv. *subito*)
mūrus, -i (masc.), *wall* — Fr. *mur*; Eng. *mural*
jacio,[2] -ere, jēci, jactum, *throw, hurl* — Eng. *reject*

III

manus, -ūs (fem.), *hand, handful (of men)* — Fr. *main*; Eng. *manual*
porto, -āre, -āvi, -ātum, *carry, convey* — Fr. *porter*
porta, -ae (fem.), *door, gate* — Fr. *porte*
quaero, -ere, quaesīvi, -ītum, *seek, look for, ask*
relinquo, -ere, -līqui, -lictum, *leave, abandon* — Eng. *derelict*
paro,[3] -āre, -āvi, -ātum, *get ready, prepare*

1 Note also: *regredior*, retire, withdraw; *ingredior*, go in, enter. (These are compounds of *gradior*.)

2 Note the compounds: *injicio*, throw in, on; *projicio*, throw forward; *dejicio*, throw away, cast aside; *abjicio*, throw away (esp. *spem abjicere*, lose hope).

3 Note the compound: *comparo*, make ready.

IV. THE STORY OF ROMULUS AND REMUS

Amulius usurped the throne of Alba from his brother Numitor; but Numitor's twin grandsons miraculously escaped the usurper's attempt to drown them.

Frātre ex Albā **pulsō**, Amūlius **sōlus** regnāvit. Tum addidit scelerī scelus. Nam duōs puerōs, quī ex fīliā frātris nascuntur, in Tiberim fluvium immittit. Sed puerī, fluviō dēlātī, in rīpam expōnuntur, et, propter sōlitūdinem territī, clāmāre incipiunt. **Clāmōrēs** eōrum audit lupa; et ex montibus, quī circā erant, statim dēscendit. Puerōs vērō nōn dēvorat; sed eōs magnā cūrā fovet, lacte nūtrit, sub **arbore** vīcīnā **pōnit**. Quōs proximō diē pastor invēnit; statim eōs **tulit** ad uxōrem suam (cūjus infans tum forte est mortuus) et per multōs annōs domī ēducāvit.

V. THE FOUNDING OF ROME

Romulus and Remus founded Rome on the site of the Seven Hills; but as the result of a foolish quarrel Remus was killed.

Rōmulus Remusque in **eōdem** locō, ubi erant expositī, urbem condere incēpērunt; sed **uterque** suum nōmen urbī novae dare volēbat. Itaque **orta** est inter cīvēs magna dis-

pello,[1] -ere, pepuli, pulsum, *drive, urge*	Eng. *compulsion*
sōlus (adj.), *alone, only*	Fr. *seul*; Eng. *sole*
clāmor, -ōris (masc.), *noise, shout*	Eng. *clamour*
arbor, -oris (fem.), *tree*	Fr. *arbre*
pōno, -ere, posui, -itum, *place, put, set, put down*	Eng. *position*
fero,[2] ferre, tuli, lātum, *bring, carry, endure*	Eng. *refer, ablative*

V

īdem (pron.), *same*	Eng. *identity*
uterque (pron.), *both, each (of two)*	
orior, -īri, ortus, *arise, get up*	Eng. *Orient*[3]

[1] Note the compounds: *expello*, drive out; *impello*, drive on, urge; *compello*, force, compel; *depello*, drive away; *repello*, repulse; *appello*, direct (a ship) to shore.

[2] Note the compounds: *offero*, offer; *affero*, bring to; *refero*, bring back, report, tell.

[3] Why does this mean the East?

cordia; nam aliī Rōmulō, aliī Remō favēbant. Deinde frātrēs in **montem**, quī prope erat, ascendērunt, augurium petentēs. Sex vulturēs vīdit Remus, sed duōdecim Rōmulus; cuī propter numerum **avium populus** regnum dedit. Haec rēs mōvit Remī invidiam; quī novōs mūrōs contemnere incēpit. 'Hīsne', inquit, '**tūtus** erit populus?' et mūrum insolenter transiluit. Tum Rōmulus, īrā mōtus, frātrem rastrō (*rake*) necāvit; quō factō, regnum sōlus tenēbat.

VI. THE REIGN OF ROMULUS

Romulus collected men from neighbouring tribes to populate the city and found them wives by seizing the maidens of the friendly Sabines at a festival.

Rōmānum Imperium ex Rōmulō orīginem habet. Conditā urbe, quam ex nōmine suō Rōmam vocāvit, haec fēcit. Multitūdinem vīcīnōrum in **cīvitātem** recēpit. Tum centum virōs ex seniōribus ēlēgit, quōs propter senectūtem 'senātōrēs' nōmināvit; et hōrum consiliō omnia facere solēbat. Deinde, quod uxōrēs **ipse** et populus nōn habēbant, invītāvit ad spectāculum lūdōrum vīcīnās nātiōnēs, et eārum virginēs rapuit. Inceptō propter **injūriam** bellō, Sabīnōs et aliās nātiōnēs vīcit. Tandem, ortā subitā **tempestāte**, Rōmulum **nēmo** reperīre poterat. Nam, ut crēdunt Rōmānī, ad deōs immortālēs ascenderat.

mons, -tis (masc.), *mountain* — Fr. *mont*
avis, -is (fem.), *bird*
populus, -i (masc.), *people, populace* — Fr. *peuple*
tūtus (adj.), *safe, protected*

VI

cīvitas, -ātis (fem.), *state, country*. (Root: *cīvis*, a citizen)
ipse (pron.), *self*
injūria, -ae (fem.), *harm, wrong, injury*
tempestas, -ātis (fem.), *storm, tempest*
nēmo, (Gen.: use nullius) (pron.), *no one, nobody*

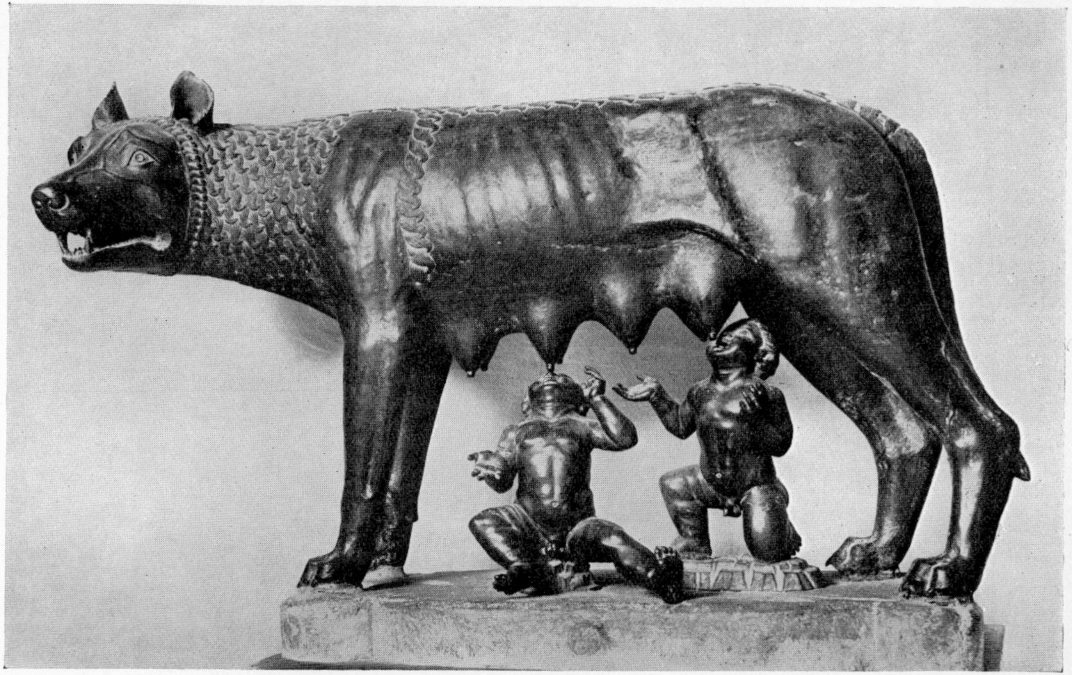

Photo Anderson

ROMULUS, REMUS AND THE WOLF

VII. A MORTAL COMBAT

Tarquin the Proud, when expelled from Rome, enlisted the aid of the Etruscan King, Lars Porsenna. As he approached the city with the Etruscan host, the following incident occurred.

Ubi hostēs in agrum Rōmānum perveniunt, consulēs exercitum ad pugnam parant. Valĕrius peditēs dūcit; Brūtus cum equitibus antecēdit. Hostium equitibus praeest Arruns Tarquinius, fīlius rēgis; rex ipse cum legiōnibus **sequitur**. Tum, **aciē** ad proelium nōndum instructā, **appropinquāvit** Arruns ad **agmen** Rōmānōrum; inter quōs ubi Brūtum faciē cognōverat, 'Ille est vir', inquit, 'quī nōs expulit **patriā**'; et, concitātō calcāribus (*spurs*) equō, in consulem ruit. Nec Brūtus impetum immōtus **exspectat**; summā ferōcitāte ambō concurrunt; et uterque, alterīus hastā transfixus, moriens ex equō lapsus est.

VIII. HORATIUS KEEPS THE BRIDGE

The Etruscan attack on Rome was continued, but was repulsed through Horatius' defence of the bridge across the Tiber.

Etruscōrum adventū nuntiātō, Rōmānī in urbem ex agrīs fugiunt; et **pontem** ferrō atque **igne** perrumpere incipiunt. Intereā Horātius Coclēs, in ponte positus, impetum hostium cum Spŭriō Larciō āc Tĭtō Herminiō **sustinet**. Mox hōs trans pontem redīre jussit; et ipse, circumferens trucēs oculōs, hostibus sōlus resistit. Etruscī, clāmōre sublātō, hastīsque ex omnibus partibus conjectīs, eum dējicere

sequor, -i, secūtus, *follow, pursue* — Eng. *sequence*
acies, -ei (fem.), *line of battle, array*
appropinquo, -āre, -āvi, -ātum, *approach, come near*
agmen, -inis (neut.), *army on the march, line of march*
patria, -ae (fem.), *fatherland, native country* — Fr. *patrie*
exspecto, -āre, -āvi, -ātum, *wait for, await* — Eng. *expect*

VIII

pons, -tis (masc.), *bridge* — Fr. *pont*
ignis, -is (masc.), *fire*
sustineo,[1] -ēre, -ui, -tentum, *hold up, withstand* — Eng. *sustain*

[1] This is a compound of *sub* and *teneo*.

cōnantur. Subitō audītur fragor ruptī pontis. Tum Coclēs, 'Tiberīne pater,' inquit, 'mē propitiō **flūmine** accipe.' Quibus dictīs, armātus in Tiberim dēsiluit, et **incolumis** ad suōs transnāvit.

IX*a*, *b*. A POLITICAL STRIKE

The Plebeians formed an important part of the Roman army; and, when they went 'on strike' and 'seceded' to the Sacred Mount, it was a critical moment for the state.

IX*a*

Hōc tempore magna fuit in urbe discordia. Nam violentia consulum īram plēbēiōrum mōvit. Plēbēī igitur prīmum dē caede consulum dēlīberant; deinde, suādente Siciniō, multī urbem relinquunt et, arma ferentēs, ad Sacrum Montem sēcēdunt. Ibi, castrīs **fossā vallō**que mūnītīs, per multōs diēs quiescunt. Intereā Rōmae fit ingens tumultus. Plēbēī enim quī in urbe jam **morantur**, dē sēcessiōne dēlīberare incipiunt; quā rē exterritī Patriciī condiciōnēs pācis offerre **constituunt.** Itaque ad castra missus est Agrippa, vir ēloquens et plēbēīs cārus; quī, ad Sacrum Montem prōgressus, hōc **modō** est **locūtus**:—

IX*b*

'Corpus Hūmānum multa habet membra, inter quae sunt Manūs, Ōs, Dentēs et Venter. Inter haec membra ōlim fuit discordia. Nam Dentēs dixērunt, "**Cibum** ab Ōre acceptum

cōnor, -āri, -ātus, *try, attempt, endeavour*
flūmen, -inis (neut.), *river.* (Root: *fluo*, flow)
incolumis (adj.), *safe, unharmed, sound*

IX*a*

fossa, -ae (fem.), *ditch, trench* — Eng. *Fosse Way*
vallum, -i (neut.), *rampart* — Eng. *wall*
moror, -āri, -ātus, *delay, wait*
constituo, -ere, -ui, -ūtum, *decide, arrange, make up one's mind (to)*
modus, -i (masc.), *way, method, limit* — Fr. *mode*
loquor, -i, locūtus, *talk, say* — Eng. *elocution*

IX*b*

cibus, -i (masc.), *food*

Photos German Institute Rome

PATRICIANS AND PLEBEIANS

FROM THE ARA PACIS

mordēre nōlumus." Tum Ōs, "Cibum ā Manū adlātum ego nōn accipiam." Tum Manus, "Ego cibum ad Ōs nōn adferam." Itaque Venter alī nōn poterat, et ob discordiam inter membra sīc ortam Corpus ipsum periit. Nōlīte, O cīvēs, per vestram discordiam cīvitātem eōdem modō **perdere**.'

Hīs verbīs audītīs, plēbēīs **placuit** condiciōnēs pācis accipere. Itaque duō tribūnī sunt **creātī**, ēlectī ex **numerō** plēbēiōrum; et hī magistrātūs contrā violentiam consulum cīvibus **auxilium** ferre solēbant.

X. AN UNJUST JUDGE

Appius Claudius and nine others were appointed, as 'decem-viri', to draw up a code of laws. His attempt to misuse his power provoked a mutiny and he was deposed.

Appius Claudius, amōre **incensus**, Verginiam, fīliam Verginiī, in mātrimōnium dūcere voluit; sed, ubi hōc a Verginiō **impetrāre** nōn poterat, consilium cēpit ātrōcissimum. Frētus enim **potestāte** decemvirālī, constituit puellam in servitūtem damnātam, velut famulam (*slave-girl*), in domum suam abdūcere. Vocat in Forum Verginiam; lictōribus comitantibus, in tribūnal (*platform*) ascendit; jūs dīcere **coepit**. Intereā concitātur multitūdo ātrōcitāte sceleris. Adstant **flentēs** mātrōnae. Circumit Verginius ipse, auxilium **ōrans**

perdo, -ere, -didi, -ditum, *lose, destroy* — Fr. *perdre*
placeo, -ēre, -ui, -itum, *please.* (Impersonal: *placet*, it seems right, good, fit)
creo, -āre, -āvi, -ātum, *make, create*
numerus, -i (masc.), *number* — Fr. *numéro*
auxilium, -i (neut.), *help, aid, assistance* — Eng. *auxiliary*

X

incendo, -ere, -di, -sum, *burn, inflame* — Eng. *incendiary*
impetro, -āre, -āvi, -ātum, *get by asking, obtain, succeed in getting*
potestas, -ātis (fem.), *power, ability.* (Root: *possum*=*pot-sum*, I am able)
coepi, -isse (perfect: present not found), *began, started*
fleo, -ēre, flēvi, -ētum, *weep, lament*
ōro, -āre, -āvi, -ātum, *ask, request, beg* — Eng. *oratory*

et dē violentiā decemvirī **querens.** Tandem, ubi nullam spem vīdit, 'Ignosce, O Appī,' inquit, 'dolōrī paternō; sinās mē **semel** fīliam meam complectī.' Dein, veniā datā, eam ad tabernās vīcīnās sēduxit; et, ā laniō (*butcher*) cultrō (*knife*) abreptō, clāmāvit, 'Hōc unō modō possum te līberāre', et pectus puellae transfixit.

XI. CINCINNATUS

In times of crisis the consuls were often replaced by a single commander-in-chief or dictator. *The simple rustic character of the early Romans is well illustrated by this story.*

Tum Rōmae magna fuit trepidātio; et, omnī spē auxiliī āmissā, cīvēs dē **salūte** rēīpublicae dēspērāre incipiēbant. Placuit igitur senātōribus dictātōrem creārī; et omnium consensū ēlectus est Lūcius Quintius Cincinnātus, vir summae **virtūtis** et industriae. Is **paucīs** ante annīs consul fuerat; sed post consulātum sē vītae rusticae dederat, et agrum procul ab urbe trans Tiberim colēbat. Ibi lēgātī, ā senātū missī, eum reperiunt fossam fodientem, sūdōre fluentem, et (nam **aestās** forte erat) sēminūdum. Salūtant eum lēgātī; sed, sīc nūdum videntēs, dē dictātūrā **silent.** Is, salūtātiōne redditā, **uxōrem** jubet togam ē domō adferre; sūdōrem absterget (*wipe off*); et togam adlātam induit, **iterum** iterumque rogitans 'Suntne omnia domī salva?' Tum eī togātō congrātulantur lēgātī; omnia, quae senātus jusserat, nuntiant; et Quintium, lictōribus comitantibus, ad urbem dēdūcunt.

queror, -i, questus, *complain, grumble* — Eng. *querulous*
semel (adv.), *once*

XI

salus, -ūtis (fem.), *safety, security*
virtus, -ūtis (fem.), *manliness, courage, bravery* — Eng. *virtue*
pauci (adj.), *few*
aestās, -ātis (fem.), *summer* — Fr. *été*
sileo, -ēre, -ui, *be quiet, say nothing* — Eng. *silent*
uxor, -ōris (fem.), *wife*
iterum (adv.), *again, a second time*

XII. CORIOLANUS

The Roman general Coriolanus was driven into exile; but he joined the Volscians and, being given command of their army, led them against his own city.

Coriolānus, cum exercitū Volscōrum **profectus**, castra prope urbem posuit. Stupēbant senātōrēs; trepidābat populus; virī fēminaeque spem salūtis nullam habēbant. Decem lēgātī, condiciōnēs pācis ferentēs, ab hostibus nōn recipiuntur. Sacerdōtēs quoque, vestibus sacrīs vestītī, Coriolānum ipsum petunt; sed **animum** ējus movēre nōn possunt. Tum, mātrōnīs **suādentibus**, Veturia, māter Coriolānī, cum uxōre līberīsque ējus castra petunt. Quās procul conspicātus quīdam Coriolānō nuntiāvit, 'Mātrem tuam cum uxōre **līberīs**que appropinquantem videō.' Deinde Coriolānus, ex sēde ortus, ad suōs currit; cuī venientī exclāmat māter 'Dīc mihi hōc ūnum! Utrum ad fīlium veniō an ad hostem?' Sīc locūta, manūs eī extendit; et līberī, ante **pedēs** ējus lapsī, **lacrimās** fundunt. Tandem Coriolānus, precibus lacrimīsque mōtus, dixit: 'Mē vīcistī, O māter. Patriam **servāvistī**; sed fīlium perdidistī.' Tum, suōs complexus, et ad Volscōs regressus, castra statim movērī jussit.

XIII*a*, *b*. THE GAULS TAKE ROME

The Gauls took possession of the city, but were foiled in their attempt to seize the Capitol or citadel.

XIII*a*

Clāde nuntiātā, aliī per agrōs fūgērunt, aliī urbēs vīcīnās petiērunt. Juventus mīlitāris senātūsque **rōbur** cum uxōri-

proficiscor, -i, -fectus, *set out, start*
animus, -i (masc.), *mind, intention*
suādeo,[1] -ēre, suāsi, -sum, *urge, encourage* — Eng. *persuasion*
līberi, -ōrum (masc.), *children*
pēs, pedis (masc.), *foot* — Eng. *pedal*
lacrima, -ae (fem.), *tear*
servo, -āre, -āvi, -ātum, *save, keep* — Eng. *preservation*

XIII *a*

rōbur, -oris (neut.), *strength.* (Lit. the hardwood at the centre of an oak-tree)

[1] Note also: *persuadeo*, urge successfully, persuade.

bus līberīsque in arcem ascendērunt ut sē **ibi** omnī modō dēfenderent. Seniōrēs quīdam, domōs regressī, obstinātō ad **mortem** animō hostium adventum exspectābant. Posterō diē Gallī, quum in urbem, **patente** Collīnā portā, pervēnissent, oculōs circumferentēs nēminem vidēre poterant. Deinde, sōlitūdine exterritī, in Forum ipsum prōcēdunt; ubi inveniunt in domōrum vestibulīs sedentēs virōs quī mājestāte ōrisque gravitāte **simillimī** deōrum simulācrīs videntur. Ūnus ex hīs, nōmine Papīrius, Gallum barbam suam permulcentem (*stroking*) baculō eburneō incutit. Deinde illum in sēde statim trucīdant Gallī, neque **cuīquam cēterōrum** parcunt. Tecta ubīque dīripiuntur, dīreptīsque ignēs injiciuntur.

XIII*b*

Intereā iī quī Capitōlium tenēbant in magnō **perīculō** fuērunt. Nam Gallī, quum in arcem impetum facere constituissent, silentiō noctis **clam** ascendērunt. Nōn tamen fefellērunt anserēs sacrōs, quī in Jūnōnis templō **alēbantur**; quae rēs salūtī fuit. Namque, clangōre avium **excitātus**, Marcus Manlius, armīs raptīs, vādit; et, dum cēterī trepidant, Gallōrum ducem trucīdat. Deinde aliī concurrentēs hastīs **saxīs**que hostēs dējiciunt. Mox Gallī, magnō aurī **pondere** acceptō, ab urbe dēcēdere voluērunt.

ibi (adv.), *there*	
mors, -rtis (fem.), *death*	Fr. *mort*; Eng. *mortal*
pateo, -ēre, -ui, *be open, be obvious*	Eng. *patent*
similis (adj.), *like, alike*	Eng. *similar*
quisquam[1] (pron.), *anyone*	
cēteri (adj.), *the rest, the others*	Eng. *etcetera*

xiii*b*

perīculum, -i (neut.), *danger, risk*	Eng. *peril*
clam (adv.), *secretly*	
alo, -ere, -ui, altum, *feed, nourish*	Lat. *altus*[2]
excito, -āre, -āvi, -ātum, *rouse, excite*	Fr. *exciter*
saxum, -i (neut.), *rock, boulder*	
pondus, -eris (neut.), *weight, mass*	Eng. *ponderous*

[1] *quisquam* occurs only after a negative.

[2] *altus*, really a participle, means 'well nourished'; so 'tall'; and so also 'deep'.

XIV*a*, *b*. A ROMAN ARMY TRAPPED

The Samnites, who dwelt among the mountains of central Italy, were Rome's most stubborn enemy. On this occasion they lured her army into an ambush near a ravine called the Caudine Forks.

XIV*a*

Jacet inter duās **angustiās** campus herbidus et aquōsus; per quem medium **iter** est. Quō quum Rōmānī pervēnissent, viam arboribus saxīsque saeptam (*blocked*) invēnērunt, et armātōs locum undique obsidentēs vīdērunt. Tum inter sē dīcunt hostēs sibi **insidiās** parāre neque ullam esse **spem** fugae. Impetū factō, nihil efficere poterant. Consulēs igitur, pācem petentēs, prōmīsērunt sē arma hostibus trāditūrōs et ex agrīs eōrum esse abitūrōs. Quibus **condiciōnibus** acceptīs, dux Samnītium exercitum Rōmānum sub **jugum** īre coēgit. Prīmum consulēs cum singulīs vestibus sub jugum mittuntur. Mīlitēs inermēs et sēminūdī sequuntur. Circumstant armātī hostēs, aliōs vōce insultantēs, aliīs gladiōs intentantēs. Ita vultū tristī animōque dēmissō domum **miserī redeunt.**

XIV*b*

Intereā Rōmae summa est cīvium **īra**, summus pudor. Dēclārant omnēs rem esse **turpissimam**; vix **crēdunt** exercitum arma hostibus **trādidisse.** Multī dīcunt mīlitēs

angustiae, -ārum (fem.), *narrows, pass, defile*
iter, -ineris (neut.), *journey, route, way* — Eng. *itinerary*
insidiae, -ārum (fem.), *ambush, trap* — Eng. *insidious*
spes, spei (fem.), *hope, expectation*
condicio, -iōnis (fem.), *term, condition*
jugum, -i (neut.), *yoke, ridge.* (Root: *jungo*, join)
miser (adj.), *wretched, unhappy, miserable*
redeo,[1] -īre, -īvi, -itum, *go back, return*

xiv*b*

īra, -ae (fem.), *anger, wrath*
turpis (adj.), *base, foul, disgraceful*
crēdo, -ere, crēdidi, -itum, *entrust* (+acc.); *believe* (+dat.) — Eng. *credit*
trādo,[2] -ere, -didi, -ditum, *hand over, hand down, surrender* — Eng. *tradition*

[1] This is a compound of *re* and *eo*, go ('d' for sound). Note also: *abeo*, depart, go away; *adeo*, approach.

[2] This is a compound of *trans* and *do*. Compare: *reddo*, give back, return; *ēdo*, give forth, produce; *abdo*, hide.

propter ignāviam suppliciō dignōs fore. Quī quum ad portās urbis pervēnissent, Forum dēsertum, tabernās **clausās** vīdērunt. Noctū igitur ingressī in suīs **quisque** domibus sē clam abdidērunt. Proximō diē senātōrēs dē pāce dēlīberāvērunt; condiciōnēs quās consulēs accēperant, nōn approbāvērunt; negant sē eās accipere velle. Itaque consulēs **vinctōs** ad hostium castra remīsērunt.

XV. AN INCORRUPTIBLE ROMAN

Pyrrhus defeated Rome's army more than once, yet could not force her to terms. So he tried to bribe her ambassador—but in vain.

Mīrā fuit constantiā Gaius Fabricius, vir in rēbus vel prosperīs vel adversīs constantissimus. Hunc ā senātū **missum** Pyrrhus magnificō hospitiō accēpit; spērāvit enim sē eum corrumpere posse. Itaque multa dōna, dein magnum pondus aurī, dēnique partem regnī suī eī obtulit. Quibus rēbus nēquāquam mōtus, Fabricius rēgī **respondit** 'Si mē malum esse crēdis, **cūr** vīs amīcitiam meam? sī bonum, cūr mē corrumpī posse spērās?' Proximō diē **alterum** consilium cēpit Pyrrhus. Nam, elephantō post aulaeum (*curtain*) clam positō, Fabricium ad sē vocāvit. Paulisper colloquuntur; nihil suspicātur Fabricius; tum subitō, dīductō aulaeō, elephantus super **caput** Fabriciī manum (*trunk*) dēmīsit fremitumque horribilem ēdidit. Fabricius, nōn exterritus, sē **vertit**; et rīdens, 'Vidēs', inquit, 'mē neque herī aurō tuō corruptum neque **hodiē** bestiā territum.'

claudo, -ere, -si, -sum, *shut, close* — Eng. *clause*
quisque (pron.), *each*
vincio, -īre, -nxi, -nctum, *bind, imprison, enchain* — Lat. *vinculum*

XV

mitto, -ere, mīsi, missum, *send* — Eng. *mission*
respondeo, -ēre, -di, -sum, *answer, reply* — Fr. *répondre*
cūr (adv.), *why*
alter (pron.), *the one, the other, second*
caput, -itis (neut.), *head* — Eng. *capital*
verto, -ere, verti, versum, *turn* — Eng. *version*
hodie (adv.) (*hoc die*), *to-day*

XVI. A STRANGE ENCOUNTER

Regulus' army, when landed on the coast of Africa, met (so legend tells) with a formidable monster of the desert.

Rēgulus, iter cum exercitū faciens, haud **procul** ā flūmine Bagradā castra posuit. Mīlitibus vērō ad aquam dēscendentibus occurrit serpens **mīrae** magnitūdinis; quae aliōs fugāvit, aliōs captōs dēvorāvit. Ferunt nātūram serpentis **tālem** fuisse. Pedibus **carēbat**: sed squāmīs (*scales*), quās in ventre habēbat, velut pedibus ūtēbātur; neque per plāna sōlum, sed etiam per **rūpēs** atque montēs lābī solēbat. Tum Rēgulus, quum **cognōvisset** mīlitēs suōs in magnō perīculō stāre, contrā bestiam cum exercitū tōtō est profectus; sed in **tergum** ējus hastās conjicientēs, corpus vulnerāre nullō modō poterant. Itaque Rēgulus, quum multōs morsū, multōs hālitū (*breath*) pestiferō **morī** vidēret, ballistās (*artillery*) adferrī jussit. Dēnique serpens, saxōrum ictū concussa, exspīrāvit; et corium (*hide*) ējus (quod longitūdinem centum vīgintī pedum erat) Rōmam dēvectum, omnibus mīrāculō fuit.

procul (adv.), *afar, far off, at a distance*
mīrus (adj.), *wonderful, marvellous*
tālis (adj.), *such, of such a kind.* (Correlative: *quālis*)
careo, -ēre, -ui, *lack, be without* (with Ablative)
rūpes, -is (fem.), *rock*
cognosco,[1] -ere, -nōvi, -nitum, *get to know, learn, discover* Eng. *recognition*
tergum,[2] -i (neut.), *back*
morior, -i, mortuus, *die* Fr. *mourir*

[1] Note also: *agnosco*, recognise.
[2] Note the phrases: *a tergo*, in the rear; *terga vertere*, to turn in flight.

XVII. A TRUE PATRIOT

Among all the tales of Roman heroism none was more famous than that of Regulus. Captured by the Carthaginians and sent to Rome with an offer of terms, he refused to recommend these and rather than break his parole returned to captivity and death in Africa.

Rōmānōs, quamquam in prīmō proeliō rem bene **gessērunt**, mox fortūna dēseruit. Nam Poenī, duce Xanthippō (qui ā Lacedaemoniīs missus est), eōs proximō annō **vīcērunt** et Rēgulum ipsum captum in **carcerem** conjēcērunt. Paucīs post annīs Poenī, multīs **cāsibus** fractī, pācem ā senātū petere constituērunt; et ob hanc causam Rēgulum Rōmam mīsērunt. Quī quum in Cūriam vēnisset, senātōribus ita locūtus est: 'Nōlīte, O patrēs, condiciōnēs vel accipere vel offerre; scītis enim hostēs decēre potius victōriam quam pācem petere.' Haec locūtō suāsērunt **amīcī** ut in urbe manēret nēve ad Africam redīret. Sed ille negāvit sē **manēre** posse; nolle enim ea, quae Poenīs prōmīsisset, violāre. Itaque ad Africam regressus, in potestātem hostium sē rursus trādidit; ubi **crūdēlī** suppliciō periisse dīcitur.

XVIII. LAKE TRASIMENE

Hannibal, finding that he could not draw Flaminius, the Roman general, into battle, marched past him along the road to Rome, and laid an ambush by the shore of the lake.

Hīc via est perangusta; ex alterā parte patescit **lacus**, ex alterā montēs insurgunt. Hannibal peditēs in montibus instruit, equitēs ad ipsās faucēs locat. Postrīdiē prīmā **lūce**

gero,[1] -ere, gessi, gestum, *carry, conduct, perform* — Eng. *digestion*
vinco, -ere, vīci, victum, *conquer, overcome* — Fr. *vaincre*; Eng. *victory*
carcer, -is (masc.), *prison, gaol*
cāsus, -ūs (masc.), *chance, accident, misfortune* — Eng. *case*
amīcus, -i (masc.), *friend* — Fr. *ami*
maneo, -ēre, -nsi, -nsum, *remain, stay* — Eng. *mansion*
crūdēlis (adj.), *cruel, heartless*

XVIII

lacus, -ūs (masc.), *lake* — Fr. *lac*
lux, lūcis (fem.), *light*

[1] Note the phrase: *bellum gerere*, to wage war.

Flāminius, insidiās nōn suspicātus, ad lacum appropinquat; locum nōn explōrat; hostēs nebulā tectōs nōn videt; **vōcem** nullam audīre poterat. Subitō dux Poenōrum **signum** invādendī suīs dat. Dein, ortō undique clāmōre, Rōmānī sē circumventōs esse intellegunt; nam et ā fronte et ā tergō hostium aciēs eōs claudit. Trēs **hōrās** ācriter pugnātum est; circum consulem tamen **ācrior** pugna est. Tandem Rōmānōrum fuga coepit; et jam nec lacus nec montēs pavōrī obstābant. Nulla tamen facultās effugiendī datur. Per vada **palūdis** in aquam prōgressī, sē umerīs tenus immergunt. Multī aut hauriuntur gurgitibus aut vada fessī repetunt, ubi ab hostium equitibus trucīdantur. Dēnique, incalescente (*growing hot*) **sōle**, dispellitur nebula; et montēs campīque strātam ostendunt Rōmānam aciem.

XIX. THE NEWS AT ROME

The cool courage, with which the Senate met this and other defeats, ensured the ultimate success of the Roman arms.

Rōmae, nuntiātā clāde, cum **ingentī** terrōre āc tumultū populus in Forum concurrit; tum, in Cūriam versus, magistrātūs magnā vōce **appellāvit.** Tandem, sōle occidente, Marcus Pompōnius, **cōram** populō prōgressus, 'Pugnā', inquit, 'magnā victī sumus.' Dein, quamquam nihil aliud ex eō audīverant, domum regressī, rūmōrēs variōs spargere incēpērunt 'consulem cum magnā parte exercitūs esse

vox, vōcis (fem.), *voice* — Fr. *voix*
signum, -i (neut.), *signal, standard* — Eng. *sign*
hōra, -ae (fem.), *hour* — Fr. *heure*
ācer (adj.), *keen, eager.* (Adv. *ācriter*)
palus, -ūdis (fem.), *marsh, swamp*
sōl, -is (masc.), *sun* — Eng. *solar*

XIX

ingens (adj.), *huge, vast, large*
appello, -āre, -āvi, -ātum, *call, summon* — Fr. *appeler*
cōram (adv.), *publicly*; (prep.+abl.), *in the presence of*

interfectum: superesse paucōs **aut fugā** sparsōs **aut** ab hostibus captōs: Poenōs ad urbem mox adfutūrōs esse'. Proximō diē ab ortō sōle ad occidentem senātōrēs, in Cūriam convocātī, dēlīberābant. Tandem, populō approbante, dictātor creātus est Quintus Fabius Maximus; quī senātūs jussū mūrōs **turrēs**que firmāvit, **praesidia** disposuit, pontēsque flūminum perrūpit.

XX. HANNIBAL AT THE GATES

After many victories Hannibal still found that Rome would not yield. So eventually he marched on the city, hoping to produce panic among the citizens—but in vain.

Dum exercitus Poenōrum per agrōs Latīnōs prōgreditur, magnam turbam agrestium subitus terror in urbem compulit. Hannibal, quum tria **mīlia** passuum ab urbe aberat, castra prope Aniēnem (*Anio*) fluvium posuit. Nam propter cīvium terrōrem sē urbem captūrum esse spērāvit. Minuērunt tamen spem ējus duae rēs. Rōmānī enim, **quamquam** hostēs prope moenia urbis armātī **sedēbant, novās** cōpiās ad Hispāniam mittere ausī sunt. Altera rēs minor erat; sed constantiam cīvium etiam magis dēmonstrāvit. Nam illō tempore vēniit (*was put on sale*) in urbe ager, in quō Poenī castra posuerant; sed nōn ob hanc causam **pretium** agrī dēminūtum est. Id **superbum** et indignum Hannibālī

interficio, -ere, -fēci, -fectum, *kill, slay*
aut (adv.), *or* (*aut*...*aut*, either...or)
fuga, -ae (fem.), *flight*
turris, -is (fem.), *tower, turret*
praesidium, -i (neut.), *guard, garrison, defence*

XX

mille (adj.), *thousand* — Fr. *mille*; Eng. *mile*[1]
quamquam (conj.), *although*
sedeo, -ēre, sēdi, sessum, *sit* (*encamp*) — Eng. *session*
novus (adj.), *new, fresh* — Fr. *nouveau*; Eng. *novelty*
pretium, -i (neut.), *price* — Eng. *precious*
superbus (adj.), *proud, arrogant*

[1] From *mille passūs*, a thousand paces.

vīsum est. Itaque, praecōne vocātō, tabernās circā Forō Rōmānō sitās vēnīre jussit. Tandem, quum sē Rōmam capere nōn posse **intellegeret**, ad portam ipsam equō vectus, hastam in urbem conjēcit; tum, mōtīs castrīs, exercitum in Campāniam reduxit.

XXI. BATTLE OF THE METAURUS RIVER

Hannibal's brother Hasdrubal marched from Spain with reinforcements; but on arriving in Italy he was intercepted, defeated and killed.

Hasdrubal, quum fluvium Metaurum transiisset, castrīs prope Sēnam positīs, **equitēs** quattuor cum **litterīs** ad Hannibalem mīsit; quī, ā pābulātōribus (*foragers*) Rōmānīs captī, ad consulem Gaium Claudium Nerōnem dēdūcuntur. Ille, litterīs perlectīs, perīculī magnitūdinem intellegit; et, cum parte exercitūs suī profectus, ad castra Līviī, collēgae suī, magnīs itineribus **contendit**. Cūjus dē adventū certior factus **veritus**que nē ā cōpiīs superiōribus ipse opprimerētur, Hasdrubal exercitum suum redūcere constituit. Itaque sub noctem, ignibus extinctīs vāsibusque (*baggage*) silentiō **collectīs**, castra movērī jussit. Prīmō, tenebrīs dēceptī, per agrōs errant; mox, somnō strātī, diem exspectant. Prīmā lūce rīpam fluviī explōrant, vada petentēs, sed propter ignōrantiam locī ea reperīre nōn possunt. Intereā sequuntur Rōmānī, ad proelium **instructī**, et ex omnibus partibus, ā fronte, ā latere, ā tergō impetum faciunt, permultōsque

intellego, -ere, -lexi, -lectum, *understand, realise* — Eng. *intelligent*

XXI

eques, -itis (masc.), *horseman, knight*. Pl. *equites, cavalry*

littera, -ae (fem.), *letter of the alphabet*. Pl. *letter, despatch* — Fr. *lettre*; Eng. *literal*

contendo, -ere, -tendi, -tentum, *stretch, exert one's self, march* — Eng. *contend*

vereor, -ēri, veritus, *fear, be afraid*

colligo,[1] -ere, -lēgi, -lectum, *gather together, collect*

instruo, -ere, -struxi, -structum, *draw up, arrange* — Eng. *instruction*

[1] This is a compound of *con-* and *lego*, pick, choose; read. Compare: *ēligo*, choose out, elect.

trucīdant. Hasdrubal, suōs et verbīs et exemplō diū hortātus, tandem concitātō equō in mediōs hostēs ruit et pugnans cecidit. Caput ējus, ā corpore abscissum et jussū Claudiī servātum, in castra Hannibalis jēcērunt Rōmānī: quō vīsō, Hannibal, magnō **dolōre** permōtus, 'Fortūnam', inquit, 'Carthāginis agnosco.'

XXII. HANNIBAL'S DEATH

After peace had been made between Rome and Carthage, Hannibal was exiled from his country and eventually found refuge at the court of the King of Bithynia; where, on the approach of a Roman envoy, he committed suicide to avoid capture.

Hannibalem ā Rōmānīs **fugientem** hospitiō recēpit Prūsiās, rex Bīthȳnōrum; quī, dē adventū **lēgātī** Rōmānī certior factus, **hospitem** vel **necāre** vel Rōmānīs trādere constituit. Itaque mīlitēs jussit tōtam Hannibalis **domum** custōdiīs claudere. Hannibalī nuntiātum est mīlitēs rēgiōs in vestibulō esse; sed postīcā (*postern*) portā fugere cōnātus, omnia custōdiīs claudī vīdit. Tum venēnum antea praeparātum **poposcit**; et 'Līberēmus', inquit, 'longā **cūrā** populum Rōmānum, qui mortem **senis** exspectāre nōlunt, sed lēgātum mīsērunt ut rēgem Prūsiam ad hospitis caedem impelleret.' Deinde exsecrātus in caput Prūsiae deōsque hospitālēs invocans, pōculum hausit.

trucīdo, -āre, -āvi, -ātum, *kill, slaughter*
dolor, -ōris (masc.), *pain, grief, sorrow*

XXII

fugio, -ere, fūgi, -itum, *flee, run away* (*from*) — Eng. *fugitive*
lēgātus,[1] -i (masc.), *ambassador, envoy, officer* — Eng. *legation*
hospes, -itis (masc.), *stranger, host, guest* — Lat. *hospitium*, hospitality
neco, -āre, -āvi, -ātum, *kill, slaughter, put to death*
domus, -ūs (fem.), *house, home*
posco, -ere, poposci, *ask, demand, beg*
cūra, -ae (fem.), *care, trouble, anxiety*
senex, senis (masc.), *old man* — Lat. *senātus*

[1] Properly a participle of *lēgo*, send.

XXIII. SCIPIO AND HIS ENEMIES

After Zama Scipio took part in a campaign against Antiochus, King of Syria; and his enemies seized on the suspicion that he had taken bribes from the King. At the trial he donned the crown he had worn during his triumphal procession after Zama.

Publius Cornēlius Scīpio post victōriam Zămensem magnō populī favōre fruēbātur, sed **odium** invidiamque inimīcōrum nōn ēvītāre poterat. Nam ā tribūnō accūsātus, quod **pecūniam** ab Antiochō rēge accēperat, in Forum est dēductus. Hūc **concurrit** ingens hominum multitūdo; et, silentiō factō, tribūnus longam ōrātionem habuit. Tum Scīpio, **corōnā** triumphālī capitī suō impositā, ad **rostra** ascendit; et 'O Quirītēs,' inquit, 'hōc diē contrā Hannibalem in Africā bene et **fēlīciter** pugnāvī; neque ingrātī esse **dēbēmus** prō tam clārā victōriā. Hunc igitur nebulōnem (*clown*) in Forō relinquāmus; et in Capitōlium ipsī ad templa eāmus ut Jovem cēterōsque deōs salūtēmus, et **grātiās** prō victōriā agāmus.' Quibus dictīs, Scīpio ad Capitōlium ascendit, sequente populō tōtōque senātū. Sōlus in Forō dēsertō manēbat accūsātor cum praecōne et scrībā (*clerk*); mox tamen, pudōre victus, ipse quoque cēterōs in Capitōlium secūtus est.

odium, -i (neut.), *hatred, dislike* — Eng. *odious*
pecūnia, -ae (fem.), *money* — Eng. *pecuniary*
concurro,[1] -ere, -curri, -cursum, *run together, gather* — Eng. *concourse*
corōna, -ae (fem.), *wreath, garland, crown* — Fr. *couronne*
rostrum, -i (neut.), *beak of a bird, beak of a ship*. Pl. *platform*[2]
fēlīciter (adv. of *felix*), *happily, successfully*
dēbeo, -ēre, -ui, -itum, *owe, ought* — Fr. *devoir*; Eng. *debt*
grātia, -ae (fem.), *favour, popularity, gratitude*. Pl. *thanks*[3] — Fr. *grâce*; Eng. *gracious*

[1] Note also the compounds: *occurro*, meet; *succurro*, help.
[2] Because the Speaker's Platform in the Forum at Rome was adorned with the prows of captured ships.
[3] Note the phrase: *gratias agere*, to give thanks.

XXIV. A REMEDY FOR PLAGUE

How superstitious the Romans were is shown by this story. Aesculapius, the god of healing, was supposed to appear in snake's form.

Per trēs annōs continuōs Rōmānī pestilentiā **vexābantur**, quam neque hominum neque deōrum auxilium dispellere poterat. Itaque sacerdōtēs lēgātōs mīsērunt ut ex Epidaurō, urbe Graecā, Aesculāpium **arcesserent**. Hī quum Epidaurum vēnissent, ab incolīs invītātī in templum deī intrāvērunt. Tum subitō anguis ex mediō templō prōlapsus, et ad mare **lēnī cursū** prōgressus, in nāvem Rōmānōrum conscendit. Fūgērunt nautae, spectāculī novitāte perterritī; mox anguem velut deum agnoscentēs, ē portū laetī **solvērunt**. Postquam, ventō prosperō **vectī**, Antium adpulērunt, anguis, in terram ēlapsus, templum Antiensium petiit. Metuēbant lēgātī nē in nāvem redīre nollet; sed rediit et in intimā parte nāvis sē abdidit, cibum a nautīs prōpositum accipiens. Sīc Rōmam perventum est; dein, ēgressīs in **rīpam** Tiberis lēgātīs, anguis ad insulam, in quā templum situm erat, transnāvit; et suō adventū pestilentiam dispulit.

XXV. THE LIBERATION OF GREECE

The Greeks frequently met to hold games (not unlike the Olympic Games) at the Isthmus near Corinth. Flamininus took this occasion to announce the terms of settlement made after the war against Macedon.

Non multis post diebus, ubi ad Isthmicos **ludos** omnes Graeci convenerant, Titus Quintius Flamininus condiciones pacis pronuntiare constituit. Itaque, **tubae** signo silentio

vexo, -āre, -āvi, -ātum, *trouble, harass, annoy* — Eng. *vexation*
arcesso, -ere, -īvi, -ītum, *summon, call together, send for*
lēnis (adj.), *smooth, gentle, calm* — Eng. *lenient*
cursus, -ūs (masc.), *running, course, race, voyage* — Fr. *course*
solvo, -ere, solvi, solutum, *loosen; set sail* (sc. *nāvem*); *pay* — Eng. *solution*
veho, -ere, vexi, vectum, *carry* — Eng. *vehicle*
rīpa, -ae (fem.), *bank, shore*

XXV

lūdus, -i (masc.), *game.* Pl. *Public Games*
tuba, -ae (fem.), *trumpet*

facto, praeconem haec verba magnā voce recitare jussit: 'SENATUI POPULOQUE ROMANO ET TITO QUINTIO FLAMININO PLACET OMNES GRAECIAE URBES, QUAE SUB REGNO PHILIPPI FUERUNT, LIBERAS ESSE.' Homines, magno gaudio affecti, primo siluerunt; nam ea, quae audiverant, se audivisse vix credebant. Iteratis vero verbis praeconis, **tanto** clamore caelum **compleverunt**, ut aves, quae forte supervolitabant, perterritae ad terram deciderent. Magna fit grātulatio. Nomen populi Romani laudibus extollunt. Consulem floribus cumulant, **dignum**que gratiis aeternis fore asseverant. Deinde **laetitia pleni** ad urbem quisque suam discesserunt et (si nobis **licet** scriptoribus antiquis credere) templa Flaminino velut deo dēdicaverunt.

XXVI *a*, *b*. CATO

Cato was in many ways a typical Roman—a keen farmer and a tough soldier. When elected censor, *it was his duty, amongst other things, to revise the list of senators and eject unworthy members.*

XXVI *a*

Marcus Porcius Căto asperi fuit animi, **linguae** acerbae. In patientia laboris vel perīculi alios longe superabat. In **judiciis** multos accusabat, a multis est accusatus; neque ob senectutem ēloquentiam neglegebat; nam sexto et octōgensimo anno causam pro se dixisse fertur. Res domesticas, ut ipse aliis exemplo foret, maxima parsimōnia (*economy*)

tantus (adj.), *so much, so great.* (Correlative: *quantus*) — Fr. *tant*
compleo,[1] -ēre, -ēvi, -ētum, *fill, fill up* — Eng. *complete*
dignus (adj.), *worthy, worth, deserving of*
laetitia, -ae (fem.), *joy, pleasure*
plēnus (adj.), *full* — Fr. *plein*
licet, -ēre, -uit, *it is lawful, it is allowed* — Eng. *licence*

XXVI *a*

lingua, -ae (fem.), *tongue, language* — Fr. *langue*; Eng. *linguist*
jūdicium, -i (neut.), *judgment, case, law-court* — Eng. *judicial*

[1] Compare also: *impleo*, fill.

regebat; neque aliam virtutem tanti aestimare solebat quanti abstinentiam. Nihil enim magni pretii in usu habebat, sed vestes vīlissimas, vasa e terra **ficta**, villam ne tectōrio (*plaster*) quidem ornatam. Eodem cibo, eodem vino, quo servi, utebatur. 'Si quid utile puto,' inquit, 'hoc utor; si non, hoc egeo.' Censor creatus, magna **auctoritate** apud populum **fruebatur**; atque eo magis id ēgit ut **mores** priscos revocaret, luxuriae nōbilium resisteret. Vetuit igitur **nimium** sumptum fieri vel in vestes vel in ornāmenta feminarum. Haec vero res etiam dignior admīratione videtur. Nam civem quemdam senatu movit, non aliam ob causam quam quod uxorem, filia inspiciente, est osculatus.

XXVI *b*

Vitae rusticae Cato magnopere **studebat**, 'Ex agricolis', dictitans, 'et viri multo fortissimi gignuntur et milites multo strēnuissimi'. De agricultura **librum** summa dīligentia composuit; in quo multas res, quae mentione dignae videntur, scripsit. 'Paterfamiliās, ubi ad villam venit, agros eodem die **vespere** circumeat. Vīlicum (*bailiff*) ad se vocet rogetque quid operis factum sit. Si vilicus dicit tempestates malas fuisse, eum ad **rationem** operum revocet. Videat quibus diebus hortum fodi, viam publicam **muniri**, vepres (*brambles*) recīdi oporteat. Vilicus sobrius fiat, neve ad cēnam eat. Ne putet se plus domino sapere, sed, si quid

fingo, -ere, finxi, fictum, *imagine, pretend, make* — Eng. *fiction*
auctoritas, -ātis (fem.), *authority, influence*
fruor, -i, fruitus or fructus, *enjoy, take pleasure in*
mōs, mōris (masc.), *custom, habit.* Pl. *character* — Eng. *morality*
nimius (adj.), *too much, excessive*

xxvi *b*

studeo, -ēre, -ui, *devote one's self to, pay attention to, study*
liber, -ri (masc.), *book* — Fr. *livre*; Eng. *library*
vesper,[1] -is (masc.), *evening*
ratio, -iōnis (fem.), *scheme, system, reason* — Eng. *rational*
mūnio, -īre, -īvi, -ītum, *fortify*; *build (a road)* — Fr. *munir*

[1] Note the parallel form: *vespera, -ae* (fem.).

difficilius imperatur, eo magis illi **pāreat.** Neve quid, domino nesciente, faciat, neve quid pluris **emat** quam oportet. Primus cubitu (*from bed*) surgat, postremus cubitum eat.'

XXVII. FALL OF CARTHAGE

The Carthaginians defended their city with fanatical courage. Only after a long siege did the Romans succeed in carrying the successive lines of defence.

Tum Poeni, quum condiciones pacis accipere nōluissent, legatos ad Romanorum castra remiserunt; et, ut urbem suam quam fortissimē dēfenderent, omnia, quae ad militarem usum necessaria videbantur, comparare coeperant. In armorum officīnis (*factories*), **aere** ferroque **egentes,** auro et **argento** utuntur. Feminae etiam crīnes suos conferunt, ut in ballistarum (*artillery*) vincula contexantur.... Romanis vero impetum facientibus nihil obstare poterat; qui murum primum, dein secundum, **denique** tertium summa vi expugnant. Poeni vero, in arcem ipsam compulsi, ne uxores līberique in **servitutem** abstrahantur, hostibus omni modo resistunt; ac, velut bestiae morientes, se summa ferocitate defendunt, diebus noctibusque novis māchinis, novis **dolis** repugnantes. Tandem vero, de salute desperantes, domibus templisque ignem ipsi immiserunt. Multi, ne in hostium manus venirent, de muris in medias flammas se dejecerunt. Reliqui ceciderunt usque ad mortem pugnantes;

pāreo,[1] -ēre, -ui, -itum, *obey, be obedient*
emo, -ere, ēmi, emptum, *buy, purchase* — ENG. *redemption*

XXVII

aes, aeris (neut.), *bronze*
egeo, -ēre, -ui, *want, be in need of, not have*
argentum, -i (neut.), *silver, money* — FR. *argent*
dēnique (adv.), *at last, finally*
servitus, -ūtis (fem.), *slavery*
dolus, -i (masc.), *trick, deception, device, stratagem*

[1] The original meaning, 'appear', is chiefly represented by the compound *appāreo.*

neque ulli vel seniori vel infanti **pepercerunt** Romani. Incendium per dies **continuos** decem et septem vix exstingui poterat. Tota urbs est obruta. Ita Carthago, septingentensimo anno postquam est condita, periit.

XXVIII. FORCEFUL DIPLOMACY

When Antiochus of Syria invaded Egypt, the stern attitude of a Roman envoy, though unsupported by any army, induced him to desist.

Antiocho, rēgi Syriae, Alexandriam appropinquanti obviam iit legatus Romanus, nomine Popilius, vir **ingenio** severissimus; cui rex, amīcitiam populi Romani petens, dextram manum extendit. Sed eum sīc salūtare noluit Romanus, ne **forte** putaret se sine ulla condicione in amicitiam recipi posse; litterasque a senatu missas ei tradidit. His litteris perlectis, rex respondit se **discedere** velle, ut cum amicis suis **paulisper consuleret**. Tum Popilius, moram non jam tolerans, virga, quam in manu tenebat, regem circumscripsit, eumque abire **vetuit**. 'Priusquam tu ex hoc circulo exeas,' inquit, 'redde responsum quod senatui referam.' Obstupefactus tam violento imperio rex paulisper haesitavit. Dein, 'Faciam', inquit, 'quod vult senatus.' Tum **demum** Popilius dextram regi, velut socio et amico, extendit.

parco, -ere, peperci, parsum, *spare, be merciful to*
continuus (adj.), *continuous, on end, one after another*

XXVIII

ingenium, -i (neut.), *intellect, character, mind* — Eng. *ingenious*
forte (adv.), *by chance, perhaps*
discēdo, -ere, -cessi, -cessum, *depart, go away*
paulisper (adv.), *for a short time, for a while*
consulo, -ere, -ui, -sultum, (1) with acc. *consult*, (2) with dat. *consult the interests of*
veto, -āre, -ui, -itum, *forbid, command not to*
dēmum (adv.), *at last* (*tum demum*, then and not before)

XXIX. ROMAN TREACHERY

Northern Italy between the Alps and the Po was inhabited by Gauls, whom the Romans conquered soon after the Punic Wars, and whom they regarded as uncivilised beings not worthy of honourable treatment.

Lūcius Quintius consul, a senatu missus qui Galliam Cisalpinam in potestatem populi Romani **redigeret**, secum duxit uxorem; quae, ab urbe sic remota, **saepe** querebatur quod spectāculo gladiatorio non jam frui poterat. Forte epulantibus (*dining*) iis, quum vino incaluissent (*grown heated*), nuntiatum est Gallum quemdam ad castra transfugam venisse ut salutem a consule imploraret. Intrōductus in tabernāculum, per interpretem consulem alloqui coeperat multisque **precibus** uti, quibus eum ad misericordiam **flecteret**. Inter cujus verba Quintius uxori, 'Visne,' inquit, '**quoniam** spectacula gladiatoria reliquisti, hunc Gallum morientem videre?' Quum ea adnuisset, consul, **stricto** gladio qui super caput **pendebat**, loquenti Gallo primum caput percussit, dein fugientem auxiliumque eorum, qui aderant, implorantem transfixit.

XXX. TIBERIUS GRACCHUS

By his uncompromising attack on the rights of landowners, this courageous but tactless young aristocrat provoked the violent opposition of the Senate —which led to his death.

Illo die Tibĕrius Gracchus, porta domus egressus, pedem forte offendit (*struck*); quo omine **contempto**, ad Forum

redigo,[1] -ere, -ēgi, -actum, *reduce, bring back*
saepe (adv.), *often, frequently*
prex, precis (fem.), *request, entreaty, prayer*
flecto, -ere, flexi, -xum, *bend, turn* — Eng. *reflexion*
quoniam (conj.), *since, seeing that*
stringo, -ere, -nxi, strictum, *bind tightly*; *draw* (*a sword*)
pendeo, -ēre, pependi, *hang down, be suspended*

XXX

contemno, -ere, -mpsi, -mptum, *scorn, despise, look down on* — Eng. *contempt*

[1] This is a compound of *ago* (see p. 46).

progreditur. Ibi, quum in rostra ascendisset, plēbem vehementer ōravit ut vitam suam contra vim inimicorum defenderent. Mox ad Capitōlium fugientem sequebatur ingens hominum multitudo. Alii eum monuerunt ne iram patrum nimia arrogantia moveret; alii, quum caput manu **tangentem** viderent, eum regnum poscere putabant. Multi quoque affirmant eum palam dixisse 'Senatu **deleto**, omnia in potestate plebis poni **oportet.**' Interea patres, in Curiam convocati, de periculo delīberant. Omnes a consule **postulant** ut rempublicam armis servet. Tum Scipio Nāsīca, ceteros **hortatus** ut se contra hostem publicum sequantur, ex Curia currit; et, illo duce, omnes ad Capitolium properant. Fit statim ātrocissima **caedes**; in qua periit ingens Gracchianorum numerus; Tiberius ipse, fragmento subsellii (*bench*) ictus, moriens **procubuit.**

XXXI. GAIUS GRACCHUS AND THE ITALIANS

In this speech Gaius Gracchus describes incidents in which Roman aristocrats disgracefully ill-treated Italian allies.

Vos oro et obsecro, O Quirītes, ne audaciam atque arrogantiam nobilium diutius toleretis; quarum magnitudinem vobis ex duobus exemplis ostendam. **Nuper** enim adulescens, nobili **genere** ortus, per Italiam iter faciens, in lectīca (*litter*) ferebatur. Ei prope Venŭsiam eunti **agrestis** qui-

tango, -ere, tetigi, tactum, *touch* — Eng. *contact*
dēleo, -ēre, -ēvi, -ētum, *blot out, destroy* — Eng. *delete*
oportet, -ēre, -uit, *it is right* (*it behoves*), (*oportet eum*, he ought; + infin. or *ut*)
postulo, -āre, -āvi, -ātum, *ask, demand*
hortor, -āri, -ātus, *urge, encourage* — Eng. *exhortation*
caedes, -is (fem.), *disaster, slaughter, defeat*
prōcumbo, -ere, -cubui, -cubitum, *fall, collapse*

XXXI

nūper (adv.), *recently, of late*
genus, -eris (neut.), *kind, type, sort, stock* — Fr. *genre*; Eng. *generally*
agrestis,[1] -is (masc.), *countryman, yokel*

[1] Properly an adjective, 'of the country'.

dam obviam venit, et servos ejus per jocum rogavit num mortuum ferrent. Quae quum audivisset, adulescens lecticam deponi jussit agrestemque usque ad mortem verberari. Haec quoque res mentione digna esse videtur. Consul quidam, **dum** cum uxore per Āpūliam iter facit, vespere ad oppidum Teanum pervenit; et, quum uxorem se lavare velle sciret, magistratui oppidi ad se vocato imperavit ut oppidanos e balineis quam celerrime summoveret. Descendit uxor ejus de raeda; ad balineas, servis comitantibus, processit; dein, quum multos ibi adhuc morantes **reperiret**, de mora **vehementissime** queri coeperat. Qua de re certior factus, consul ira statim flagravit; et magistratum, precantem ne quid ipse ob causam tam **levem** pateretur, saevissimo supplicio puniri jussit.

XXXII. BATTLE OF AQUAE SEXTIAE

The Teutoni, finding they could not draw the Romans into battle, marched on towards Italy; and then Marius pursued and overwhelmed them utterly.

Teutonis ad Romanorum castra appropinquantibus, Mărius suos ad pugnam exire vetuit. Discesserunt igitur barbari clamitantes 'se Italiam recto itinere petituros esse: et si quid Romani ad uxores mittere vellent, id sibi **mandarent**'. Deinde Aquas Sextias progressi, castra prope fluvium posuerunt, plaustris (ut solebant) pro vallo utentes. Hūc Romani secuti, quum fluvium ab hostibus teneri viderent, **sitim** timere coeperant et a duce postulaverunt ut **facultas** pugnandi quam celerrime sibi daretur. Quibus

dum (conj.), *while, as long as; until*
reperio,[1] -ire, repperi, repertum, *find, discover, reveal*
vehementer (adv.), *vigorously, violently* — Eng. *vehement*
levis (adj.), *light, fickle, slight* — Eng. *levity*

XXXII

mando, -āre, -āvi, -ātum, *entrust, order* — Eng. *mandate*
sitis, -is (fem.), *thirst*
facultas, -ātis (fem.), *ability, opportunity* — Fr. *facilité*; Eng. *faculty*

[1] This is a compound of *pario*, produce. Cf. also *aperio*, open, reveal.

Marius, digitum protendens, respondit 'Ēn aquam; quam **sanguine** vestro emere debetis.' Tum legiones, impetu facto, hostes a ripa fluvii pulsos usque ad castra eorum sunt prosecuti. Ibi atrocissima fuit pugnae **facies**; nam uxores barbarorum, bipennibus (*battle-axe*) gladiisque **raptis**, in mediam aciem ruunt; scuta Romanorum nudis manibus comprehendunt; omnia clamore horribili et ululatu (*howling*) complent. Postero die Marius milites, **somno** et cibo refectos, contra hostes iterum misit, hortatus ut gladiis scutisque rem comminus gererent, neve **pīlis**, ut priore die, uterentur. Ita usque ad meridiem pugnatum est; dein, sōlis calore fessi, Teutoni pedem referre coeperant; quos prosecuti Romani ad multam noctem trucīdaverunt.

XXXIII. MARIUS' ADVENTURES

Marius escaped from Rome to the Campanian coast, where he was caught and came within an ace of being executed.

Post errores varios variaque pericula Marius, ut Sullanos evītaret, in palude **latebat**, umeris tenus immersus. A pastore vero proditus et Minturnas deductus, in cavernam subterraneam et obscuram est conjectus. Non longo **spatio** temporis intermisso, miles, a magistratu missus qui eum necaret, in cavernam cum gladio descendit, ubi in **tenebris** sedebat Marius squālidus et inermis. Sed in tanto **discrimine** hunc fortissimum virum non deseruit animus; nam, quum militem intrantem gladiumque tenentem videret, **oculis** torvis inspiciens, magna voce, 'Visne', inquit,

sanguis, -is (masc.), *blood* — Fr. *sang*; Eng. *sanguinary*
facies, -ei (fem.), *face, appearance* — Fr. *face*
rapio, -ere, rapui, raptum, *seize, take hold of* — Eng. *rapture*
somnus, -i (masc.), *sleep*
pīlum, -i (neut.), *javelin*

XXXIII

lateo, -ēre, -ui, *lie hidden, be concealed, lurk* — Eng. *latent*
spatium, -i (neut.), *space, interval*
tenebrae, -ārum (fem.), *darkness, shade, shadows* — Fr. *ténèbres*
discrīmen, -inis (neut.), *crisis, danger, distinction* — Eng. *discrimination*
oculus, -i (masc.), *eye* — Eng. *ocular*

Photo Alinari

SULLA

'Gaium Marium occīdere?' Quibus verbis **attonitus**, miles gladio abjecto **tremens** fūgit; et eos, a quibus missus erat, oravit ne tantum **scelus** in talem virum admitterent. Concurrit interea magna Minturnensium multitudo; a quibus Marius non multis verbis impetravit ut libertatem sibi protinus redderent. Deinde, ne forte in potestatem Sullanorum veniret, navem statim conscendit prosperoque vento vectus ad Africam incolumis pervenit.

XXXIV*a*. SULLA'S PROSCRIPTIONS

After defeating his enemies in battle outside Rome, Sulla proceeded to the systematic slaughter of his political opponents within the city.

Dein Sulla, **simulatque** urbem victor intravit, **poenas** crudelissimas de adversariis **sumpsit**. Postero die milites mitti jussit qui captivos inermes interficerent; nam in proelio tria milia se jam dediderant. Dum haec multitudo **caeditur**, Sulla ipse in senatu orationem faciebat; sed, quum patres clamoribus morientium exterritos videret, neque vultum neque vocem **mutans** eos hortatus est ne tam levi re perturbarentur. 'Meo enim jussu', inquit, 'pauci sēditiosi puniuntur.' Tum per totam urbem fit atrocissima caedes, non Marianorum sōlum, sed multorum hominum innocentium. Per vias **vagantur** milites, alii sanguinis, alii **spoliorum** cupiditate impulsi; nec seniori vel juniori parcunt.

attonitus (part. and adj.), *amazed, astonished, thunder-struck*
tremo, -ere, tremui, *tremble, quake, be afraid* — Eng. *tremor*
scelus, -eris (neut.), *crime*

XXXIV *a*

simulatque, simulac (conj.), *as soon as*
poena,[1] -ae (fem.), *penalty, punishment* — Eng. *penal*
sumo,[1] -ere, -mpsi, -mptum, *take, take up* — Eng. *consume, assume*
caedo,[2] -ere, cecīdi, caesum, *beat, kill, slay*
mūto, -āre, -āvi, -ātum, *change, alter* — Eng. *permutation*
vagor, -āri, -ātus, *wander, stray* — Eng. *vagabond*
spolium, -i (neut.), *spoil, plunder*

[1] Note the phrase: *poenas sumere de*, exact punishment from, lit. to take up (i.e. claim) penalty from somebody.
[2] Note the very common compound: *occīdo*, kill.

Tandem Gaius Metellus, ne omnium civium fortunae in incerto diutius relinquerentur, a Sulla petiit ut finem **suppliciorum** statueret; cui respondit Sulla se tabulas proscriptorum (*proscribed*) esse **editurum**; et omnes, quorum nomina in tabulis continerentur, impune necari liciturum.

XXXIV*b*. SULLA'S PROSCRIPTIONS

Many innocent men were placed on the proscription lists and murdered for the sake of their property or from motives of personal revenge.

Tum **latior** fit pavor. Nam mittuntur qui viros līberosque in domibus latentes extrahant. Servi dominos, filii parentes ad necem tradunt; viros in uxorum gremio jugulant. Capita mortuorum, hastis praefixa, in Foro **ostendunt**. Nonnullos supplicio etiam crudeliore necant; quosdam enim, oculis effossis, amputatis manibus, exsecta lingua, **usque** ad mortem verberant. Sed hic non fuit malorum finis. Nam multi, inimicis suis ob odium privatum occisis, a Sulla impetraverunt ut nomina mortuorum tabulis adderet. Ii, qui fundos bonos vel pecuniam multam possidebant, in eodem periculo stabant: nam Sullani eos occīdere voluerunt quo ipsi **ditiores** fierent. Erat quidam, nomine Quintus Aurelius, vir innocens et quietus. Is, nihil de se timens, in Forum, ut tabulas legeret, venit; **legere** incepit; subito nomen suum in iis scriptum vidit. 'Vae (*woe!*) mihi misero!' inquit. 'Fundus meus Albanus mihi est **exitio**'; quem abeuntem

supplicium, -i (neut.), *punishment, torture*
ēdo,[1] -ere, ēdidi, ēditum, *give forth, produce, publish* — Eng. *edition*

XXXIV *b*

lātus (adj.), *broad, wide* — Eng. *latitude*
ostendo, -ere, -di, -sum, *show, reveal* — Eng. *ostensible*
usque (adv.), *all the way, constantly*
dīves, -itis (adj.), *rich, wealthy.* — Cf. 'Dives' in N.T.
lego, -ere, lēgi, lectum, *choose; read* — Eng. *lecture*
exitium, -i (neut.), *destruction, ruin, death*

[1] This is a compound of *do*, 'give'. Cf. *trādo*, hand over; *prodo*, betray; etc.

aliquis **agnovit** et, ut **praemium** per scelus **adipisceretur**, statim percussit.

XXXV. SIEGE OF JERUSALEM

The Jews stubbornly resisted Pompey's attack; and the Temple Hill was finally captured after a bitter struggle.

Pompeius, simulatque Hierosolymam (*Jerusalem*) pervenit, milites misit qui muros urbis bene explorarent. Hi tamen propter immensam rupis altitudinem facilem aditum invenire non poterant quo ad summum ascenderent. De quibus rebus certior factus Pompeius **collem**, in quo Templum est situm, obsidere constituit. Multo tempore sic consumpto, quum videret Judaeos septimo quōque die ab opere omni abstinere, eo die **aggerem** contra muros cumulari jussit. Deinde, turribus aggeri impositis māchinisque admotis, urbem **expugnare** parat. Tertio obsidionis **mense** in fanum irruptum est. Judaeorum alii repugnantes pereunt; alii se in rupes dejiciunt. **Sacerdotes**, quamquam Romanos gladiis strictis inruentes vident, tamen in sacrificiis persevērant et in ipso ministerio occiduntur. Tum Pompeius cum paucis **comitibus** in Templum ingressus (quo nemini **praeter** pontificem intrare licebat) candēlābra **aurea** saxeasque tabulas magna admīratione **spectavit**; sed propter sanctitatem loci nihil attigit. Postero die templum purgari jussit.

agnosco, -ere, -nōvi, -nitum, *recognise*
praemium, -i (neut.), *prize, reward*
adipiscor, -i, adeptus, *gain, get possession of*

XXXV

collis, -is (masc.), *hill* — Fr. *colline*
agger, -is (masc.), *mound, rampart* — Eng. *exaggerate*
expugno, -āre, -āvi, -ātum, *take by storm*
mensis, -is (masc.), *month*
sacerdos, -ōtis (comm.), *priest, priestess*
comes, -itis (comm.), *comrade, companion* — Fr. *comte*; Eng. *count*
praeter (prep. + acc.), *except, besides, beyond*
aureus (adj.), *golden, made of gold*
specto, -āre, -āvi, -ātum, *gaze at, look at* — Eng. *spectator*

XXXVI. CATILINE'S CONSPIRACY

While plotting revolution, Catiline remained in the city, until Cicero, then consul, revealed how an attack had been planned on his life; and so forced Catiline to flee to his friends in North Italy (63 B.C.).

Catilīna, quum bellum facere constituisset, Manlium in Etruriam misit, qui ex illis partibus copias compararet. **Interea** Romae ipse dies noctesque **vigilat**, armatos homines colligit, urbem incendere parat. Denique, quum Ciceronem consulem suis insidiis **obstare** videret, amicos media nocte apud se convocavit; quibus rogantibus, quid in animo jam haberet, novum consilium sēcreto explicuit. 'Māne', inquit, 'ad Ciceronem, **quasi** salutaturi, eamus; cum gladiis intrabimus in cubiculum ejus, et eum de improviso **inermem** occīdemus.' Unus vero ex amicis, insciis ceteris, hanc totam rem Ciceroni nuntiavit. Itaque illi, quum prima luce Ciceronis domum peterent, porta exclusi scelus turpissimum efficere non potuerunt....Paucis post diebus, senatu convocato, Cicero orationem habuit eloquentissimam, in quo multis argūmentis **demonstravit** quanto in periculo respublica staret. Sed, ubi ille adsedit (*sat down*), Catilina ex sede ortus primo auxilium patrum supplici voce postulavit; dein consuli multa male dicere coeperat. Obstrepunt (*cause an uproar*) omnes; hostem eum atque proditorem vocant. Tum ille furibundus (*mad with anger*) 'Quoniam ab inimicis circumvenior,' inquit, '**incendium**, quod paravi, communi ruina exstinguam.' Quibus dictis, ex **Curia** domum **erupit**, noctu paucis cum comitibus in Manlii castra profecturus.

intereā (adv.), *meanwhile, in the meantime*
vigilo, -āre, -āvi, -ātum, *be on the watch, be awake* — ENG. *vigilant*
obsto, -āre, -stiti, -stātum, *stand in the way of, block, prevent* — ENG. *obstacle*
quasi (adv. and conj.), *as if, as it were*
inermis (adj.), *unarmed, without defence, defenceless*
demonstro, -āre, -āvi, -ātum, *show, display* — FR. *montrer*
incendium, -i (neut.), *fire, blaze, burning* — ENG. *incendiary*
cūria, -ae (fem.), *court, courtyard*; esp. *the Senate House*
ērumpo,[1] -ere, -rūpi, -ruptum, *break forth, burst forth* — ENG. *eruption*

[1] This is a compound of *rumpo*, break. Cf. *corrumpo*, corrupt; *irrumpo*, burst in.

XXXVII. CLODIUS AND MILO

The rivalry between two faction-leaders Milo and Clodius came to a head when their retinues met outside Rome and Clodius was killed in the tussle.

Eo die, senatu dimisso, Mīlo domum redit; calceos (*shoes*) et vestīmenta mutat; dein, dum uxor se comparat, paulisper moratus, in raeda (*carriage*) cum ea proficiscitur. Sequitur puerorum symphōniacorum (*choir-boys*) et ancillarum **turba**; sedet ipse paenulatus (*wearing a cloak*); nihil mali in animo habet; **omnino** enim ignōrat quid inimici paraverint et quantum in periculum ipse sit venturus. Hora ferē undecima obviam it Clōdius, magno armatorum agmine comitante. Statim omnes in raedam impetum faciunt, raedarium (*driver*) occidunt. Milonem, quum de raeda **desiluisset** seque animo fortissimo defenderet, alii a tergo circumvenerunt, alii servos ejus caedere inceperunt. Hi vero, quum dominum suum occisum esse crederent, tantum scelus **ulcisci** constituerunt. Itaque Clodium ex taberna, in quam confugerat, extractum multis **vulneribus** trucīdant. Posthac corpus ejus ad urbem relatum amici in Curia posuerunt, et igne facto id cremaverunt; quo igne Curia ipsa incensa periit. Haec vero res **utrum** casu an consilio evenerit, incertum esse videtur.

XXXVIII. CAESAR AND THE PIRATES

Caesar's mettle was shown by his courageous behaviour when, as a young man, he was captured by pirates off Asia Minor.

Quam forti animo Caesar etiam in adulescentia fuerit, his ex rebus manifestum esse videtur. Anno enim **aetatis**

turba, -ae (fem.), *crowd, mob, disturbance*
omnīno (adv.), *absolutely, entirely, altogether*
dēsilio,[1] -īre, -ui, desultum, *jump down, leap down*
ulciscor, -i, ultus, *avenge, take vengeance on*
vulnus, -eris (neut.), *wound* — ENG. *vulnerable*
utrum (neut. of *uter, which of two?*), so (adv.) *whether* (to introduce first half of a double question, the second half being introduced by *an* (adv.), *or*)

XXXVIII

aetas, -ātis (fem.), *age*

[1] This is a compound of *salio*, jump. Cf. *prosilio*, jump forward.

vicensimo et sexto, Asiam nave petens, a **praedonibus** marĭtĭmis prope **insulam** Pharmacūsam est captus, diesque quadrāginta apud eos manens, arrogantiam **potius** quam obsequium (*flattery, submissiveness*) per id tempus **praestabat.** Nam, quotiens somno se dare voluerat, totiens silentium illis imperare **solebat.** Saepe quoque per jocum loquebatur, crucem illis minitans aliisque ludibriis irrīdens. Pro redemptione autem, dum vīginti talenta illi postulant, ipse promisit se quinquāginta daturum. 'Nescītis enim', inquit, 'et quem virum vos ceperitis et quanti meam salutem populus Romanus sit **aestimaturus.**' Tandem, soluta per amicos pecunia, a praedonibus liberatus Mīlētum **properat**; armatos colligit; naves comparat; praedones insequitur; ceterisque fugatis, nonnullos capit; quos omnes, ut antea praedixerat, crucibus affīgit.

XXXIX*a*. CAESAR AND BRITAIN

Caesar's interest in the habits of the islanders is shown by the following description.

Britannorum **plerique frumenta** non **serunt**, sed **lacte** et **carne** vivunt (est enim eis magnus **pecorum** numerus). **Pellibus** sunt vestiti; vitro (*woad*) quoque se pingunt, quod

praedo, -ōnis (masc.), *pirate, marauder, brigand*
insula, -ae (fem.), *isle, island* — Fr. *île*; Eng. *insular*
potius (adv.), *rather, for preference*
praesto, -āre, -stiti, -statum *or* -stitum, (1) intrans. *excel, be outstanding*; (2) trans. *show (qualities), offer*
soleo, -ēre, solitus, *be accustomed, be in the habit of*
aestimo, -āre, -āvi, -ātum, *think, think worth, value* — Eng. *estimate*
propero, -āre, -āvi, -ātum, *hurry, hasten, be quick*

XXXIX *a*

plērīque (adj.), *most, many, the majority*
frūmentum, -i (neut.), *corn, food, food-supply*
sero, -ere, sēvi, satum, *sow, plant* — Lat. *sata*, crops (in poetry)
lac, lactis (neut.), *milk*
caro, carnis (fem.), *flesh, meat* — Eng. *carni*vorous
pecus, -oris (neut.), *herd, flock*
pellis, -is (fem.), *pelt, skin, hide*

Photo Alinari

JULIUS CAESAR

caeruleum efficit colorem. Capillo sunt longo; et omnem partem corporis radunt praeter caput et labrum (*lip*) superius. Maritima pars insulae **incolitur** ab iis qui praedae causa ex Gallia transierant et permanserunt ut ibi agros colerent. Hi deos eosdem venerantur quos ipsi Galli. Nam natio Gallorum religionibus est dedita. Homines pro victimis sacrificant iisque sacrificiis praesunt Druides. Saepe **simulăcra** ingenti magnitudine parant quorum **membra** vivis hominibus complent. His simulacris succensis, homines flammis circumventi pereunt. Sic **plācari** deos immortales Galli **arbitrantur**.

XXXIX*b*. GEOGRAPHY OF BRITAIN

The geography of Britain was imperfectly grasped by the ancients.

Insula est nātūrā triquetra (*triangular*), cujus unum **latus** est contra Galliam et circa milia passuum quingenta pertinet (*stretches*). In hoc latere est Cantium, **quo** ferē omnes naves ex Gallia appelluntur. Secundum latus (cujus est longitudo septingentorum milium) ad Hispāniam et occĭdentem sōlem spectat; qua ex parte est Hībernia, multo minor quam Britannia et magno maris spatio ab ea dīvisa. In hoc mari est insula, quam vocant Mŏnam; multae quoque minores insulae ibi jacent; in quibus hieme, ut dicitur, dies continuos triginta est nox. De hac re nihil certum scimus, sed ipsi noctes breviores esse quam in Gallia videbamus. Tertio lateri (cujus est longitudo octingentorum milium) nulla est terra **contraria**; sed angulus hujus lateris ad Germāniam spectat.

incolo, -ere, -ui, -cultum, *inhabit, live in*
simulăcrum, -i (neut.), *image, statue*
membrum, -i (neut.), *limb* — Eng. *member*
plăco, -āre, -āvi, -ātum, *appease, quieten, placate*
arbitror, -āri, -ātus, *think, consider* — Eng. *arbitration*

XXXIX *b*

latus, -eris (neut.), *side, flank* — Eng. *lateral*
quo (adv.), *whither, to which place*
contrārius (adj.), *opposite, contrary*

Abundat Britannia eisdem arboribus quibus Gallia, praeter fāgum (*beech*) atque abietem (*fir*). Nascitur ibi plumbum (*lead*) album in mediterraneis locis, in maritimis ferrum, cujus parva est cōpia; aere utuntur importato. Caelum (*climate*) est temperatum, sed **imbribus foedum.**

XXXIX*c*. CAESAR'S FIRST LANDING

Caesar's landing in 55 B.C. *was stubbornly contested.*

His rebus gestis, Caesar ex Gallia solvit et hora diei quarta cum primis navibus ad Britanniam **pervenit.** Ibi hostium copias in omnibus montibus instructas vidit; unde tela ex superiore loco in **litus** dejicere poterant. Caesar igitur, lēgatis tribunisque militum convocatis, consilium suum ostendit; tum, signo dato, ancoras tollere jussit, et, milia passuum septem ab eo loco progressus, aperto litore naves constituit. Barbari vero, consilio Caesaris cognito, equites et essedarios (*charioteers*) praemiserunt; qui Romanos navibus egredi prohibebant. Naves enim propter magnitudinem ad litus appropinquare non poterant; neque milites propter **onus** armorum in aquam desilire **audebant**, sed, novo genere pugnae perterriti, paulisper morabantur.

Deinde is, qui decimae legionis aquilam (*eagle or standard*) ferebat, 'Desilīte', inquit, 'et, me duce, sequimini.' Haec magna voce locutus, se ex nave projecit atque in hostes aquilam ferre coeperat. Tum Romani ex navibus desiluerunt, et, impetu facto, Britannos in fugam verterunt.

abundo, -āre, -āvi, -ātum, *abound, be plentiful*
imber, -ris (masc.), *shower, rain*
foedus (adj.), *base, foul, ugly, unpleasant*

XXXIX *c*

pervenio, -īre, -vēni, -ventum, *arrive, come to*
lītus, -oris (neut.), *shore*
onus, -eris (neut.), *burden, weight* — ENG. *onerous*
audeo, -ēre, ausus, *dare* — LAT. *audax*, bold

XXXIX*d*. CAESAR'S SECOND LANDING

In 54 B.C. the natives organised their resistance farther inland, and were eventually forced back beyond the River Thames.

Caesar, exercitu exposito, castra in idōneo loco posuit. Tum, Quinto Atrio cum navibus relicto, ipse nocte profectus in hostium copias impetum fecit; qui, ad flumen progressi, ex superiore loco Romanos prohibere inceperunt. Ab equitibus vero **repulsi** in silvas fugerunt; et locum bene munitum **nacti** (quem, arboribus multis succisis, antea praeparaverant) se ibi defendere constituerunt. Sed milites legionis septimae, testudine* facta, locum ceperunt, paucisque vulneribus acceptis, Britannos ex silvis expulerunt. Caesar tamen, naturam loci conspicatus, eos fugientes prosequi nolebat, et milites ad castra reduxit.

Postero die, nuntiis a Quinto Atrio missis, Caesar rem **infelicissimam** cognovit: nam superiore nocte, tempestate subita orta, naves vim venti sustinere non potuerant et omnes in litore erant ejectae. Caesar igitur, legionibus revocatis, ipse ad naves quam celerrime rediit.

XL*a*. CAESAR IN GAUL

On one occasion the natives attacked a Roman camp when the bulk of the soldiers were absent on a foraging party. Those left behind were mostly on the sick-list; but one of these saved the day by his gallant example.

Hostibus omni ex parte aggredientibus, Romani portas castrorum aegre defendere poterant. Fit inter eos magna trepidatio; alii enim castra jam capta esse nuntiant, alii exercitum **imperatorem**que deletos. Barbari vero, nullum esse

repello, -ere, reppuli, repulsum, *drive back, repel*
nanciscor, -i, nactus, *acquire, get, get possession of*
infēlix (adj.), *unhappy, unfortunate, unsuccessful*

XL *a*

imperātor, -ōris (masc.), *commander, general*; sometimes *the Emperor*

* *testudo, -inis,* literally means 'a tortoise-shell', but is technically used (as here) for a 'close formation with shields interlocked overhead'.

in castris praesidium credentes, per portas perrumpere coeperunt. Erat aeger in castris relictus Publius Sextus Băculus, qui diem jam quintum cibo caruerat. Hic, de communi salute **desperans**, inermis ex tabernăculo (*tent*) prodit; videt hostes adesse et in magno rem esse periculo. Capit arma e comitibus, et in porta **consistit.** Sequentibus aliis centurionibus, paulisper hostium impetum sustinet. Deinde, gravibus vulneribus acceptis, relinquit eum animus; aegre per manus (*from hand to hand*) **tractus**, servatur. Hoc vero spatio temporis intermisso, reliqui se **confirmant** et in portis consistere audent.

XL*b*. THE REVOLT OF VERCINGETORIX

Gaul, though conquered by Caesar, was not cowed. A young native, Vercingetorix, raised a revolt which was suppressed only after a long campaign.

Vercingetorix, Arvernorum adulescens, magnam Gallorum multitudinem convocatam hortatur ut **communis** libertatis causā arma capiant. Deinde, ubi omnium consensu **imperium** ad eum delatum est, certum numerum militum civitati cuique imperat, armaque ex omnibus partibus colligi jubet. Summae diligentiae summam severitatem addit; nam crudelissimis suppliciis dubitantes **cogit.** Multos igni atque aliis tormentis necat; multos, **auribus** desectis aut **singulis**

despēro, -āre, -āvi, -ātum, *give up hope, despair* ENG. *desperate*
consisto, -ere, -stiti, *stand, halt, take up position*
traho, -ere, traxi, tractum, *pull, draw, drag*
confirmo, -āre, -āvi, -ātum, *strengthen, rally*

XL *b*

commūnis (adj.), *common, belonging to all* FR. *commun*; ENG. *communism*
imperium, -i (neut.), *power, command, empire* ENG. *imperial*
cōgo,[1] -ere, coegi, coactum, *compel, force, drive together, collect* ENG. *cogent*
auris, -is (fem.), *ear*
singuli (adj.), *one at a time, one each* ENG. *singular*

[1] This is a compound of *ago* (see p. 46).

oculis effossis, domum remittit, ut magnitudine poenae ceteros **terreat.** Interea vicos atque **aedificia** incendi jubet, ne pābulatores (*foragers*) Romanorum ex iis frumentum **tollere** possint. Quo consilio **probato**, vīginti urbes Gallorum uno die incenduntur.

XLI*a*. SIEGE OF DYRRHACHIUM

Caesar pinned Pompey's army to the coast by an encircling line of fortifications: but these were incomplete at the point where they reached the sea-shore. Pompey attacked this point from land and sea simultaneously and won a success which caused Caesar to abandon his attempt at encirclement. Here follows an incident from the battle.

In hoc **proelio** aquilifer, quum vulnus gravissimum accepisset, equites nostros conspicatus, 'Aquilam', inquit, 'et vivus multos per annos magna **diligentia** defendi et nunc moriens eādem fide Caesari reddo. Hanc, ut **dedecus** avertatis quod nunquam antea in Caesaris exercitu accidit, incolumem ad eum referte.' Hoc modo, omnibus primae cohortis centurionibus interfectis, **conservatur** aquila.

XLI*b*. PHARSALIA

After occupying Italy and defeating Pompey's supporters in Spain, Caesar crossed to Greece and there won the decisive victory of Pharsalia.

Caesar, ab Hispania regressus, in Graeciam transiit ut contra Pompeium suas copias duceret. Deinde in Thessalia

terreo, -ēre, -ui, -itum, *frighten, terrify* — ENG. *terrible*
aedificium, -i (neut.), *building* — ENG. *edifice*
tollo, -ere, sustuli, sublātum, *take up, lift, remove*
probo,[1] -āre, -āvi, -ātum, *test, prove, approve*

XLI *a*

proelium, -i (neut.), *battle*
dīligentia, -ae (fem.), *care, attention, trouble*
dēdecus, -oris (neut.), *disgrace* (opp. of *decus*, *-oris*, glory)
conservo, -āre, -āvi, -ātum, *keep, preserve, save*

[1] Notice also the compound: *approbo*, approve.

apud Pharsāliam **dimicare** paraverunt. **Nunquam** adhūc Romanae copiae majores in unum locum convenerant. Pompeius enim in acie sua quadraginta milia peditum, equites in **sinistro** cornu sexcentos, in dextro quingentos, Caesar peditum triginta milia, equites mille habuit. Pugnatum est magna contentione; tandem vero victus est Pompeius et castra ejus direpta sunt. Ipse Alexandriam profectus petiit ut a rege Aegypti ob amicitiam **pristinam** auxilium acciperet. Rex vero, fortunam magis quam amicitiam secutus, occīdit Pompeium et caput ejus ānulumque (*ring*) ad Caesarem misit. Tum Caesar, caput tanti viri intuens, etiam lacrimas **fudisse** dicitur.

XLII. CAESAR'S MURDER

Though he knew there was strong feeling against him, Caesar refused to take precautions and so fell victim to the conspiracy of Brutus and Cassius.

Idibus Martiis Caesar ob infirmam valetudinem domo exire **dubitavit**; sacrificantem enim eum haruspex (*soothsayer*) monuerat ut illo die magnum periculum **caveret.** Tandem vero, hortantibus amicis, ad senatum est progressus. Intranti homo quidam libellum dedit, in quo insidiae **conjuratorum** plane **indicabantur.** Caesar tamen, libellum **nondum** perlectum sinistra manu tenens, sine timore in-

apud (prep.+acc.) *near*; *at the house of*; *in the works of* (an author)
dīmico, -āre, -āvi, -ātum, *fight, struggle*
nunquam (adv.), *never, at no time*
sinister (adj.), *left-handed, left* — Fr. *sinistre*
pristinus (adj.), *former, previous, old*
fundo,[1] -ere, fūdi, fūsum, *pour, pour forth* — Eng. *diffuse*

XLII

dubito, -āre, -āvi, -ātum, *doubt, hesitate*
caveo, -ēre, cāvi, cautum, *take care, be careful* — Eng. *caution*
conjūratus,[2] -i (masc.), *conspirator*
indico, -āre, -āvi, -ātum, *show, point out* — Fr. *indiquer*; Eng. *indication*
nōndum (adv.), *not yet*

[1] Note the compounds: *confundo*, pour together, confuse; *effundo*, pour out.
[2] Properly a participle, 'sworn together'.

travit. Adsīdentem (*taking his seat*) conjurati circumsteterunt, **statim**que Cimber Tillius, quasi **aliquid** rogaturus, appropinquavit et togam ejus apprehendit. Quo signo dato, Casca eum vulneravit infra jugulum. Tum ex sede prosilientem ceteri, gladiis strictis, omnibus ex partibus eum sunt aggressi. Is primo vocem edidit nullam; Brūto tamen inruenti exclāmavit 'Et tu, Brute!' dein tribus et viginti vulneribus transfixus, ante Pompeii statuam **exanimus** procubuit.

XLIII. AUGUSTUS

By his modesty and good sense Augustus induced the Romans to accept him as the head of the State; and by his far-sighted policies he laid the foundations of the Imperial system.

Oculos habuit claros et nitidos, **dentes** parvos et scabros (*decayed*), nāsum a summo eminentem, capillum subflavum. Vultu erat sereno et tranquillo, statūra brevi sed decōra. A pueritia eloquentiam studiaque alia laboriosissime **exercebat**; inter amicos tamen non multo **sermone** utebatur. Gravem valetudinem per omnem vitam **patiebatur**; quam infirmitatem magna cura tuebatur. Hieme enim quattuor tunicas cum **pingui** toga gerere solebat, aestate portis apertis cubare, et, ne forte fēbre corriperetur, rarissime se lavare. Vini erat parcissimus; nec plus quam septem horas noctu dormiebat. In convīviis abstinentia potius quam luxuria utebatur. In publica quoque vita mira fuit cōmitate et modestia. Nam adūlationes immodicas ōderat; et, ut

statim (adv.), *straight away, immediately*
aliquis (pron.), *anyone, someone*
exanimus (adj.), *lifeless, dead*

XLIII

dens, -tis (masc.), *tooth* — Fr. *dent*; Eng. *dentist*
exerceo, -ēre, -ui, -itum, *exercise, practise*
sermo, -ōnis (masc.), *talk, conversation, discourse* — Eng. *sermon*
patior, -i, passus, *suffer, allow, permit* — Eng. *passive*
pinguis (adj.), *fat, rich, thick*

salutationes vulgi **vitaret**, lectīca (*litter*) clausa iter saepe faciebat. Olim, quum quemdam libellum sibi magna haesitatione dare videret, 'Cur sic haesitavisti,' inquit, 'quasi elephanto stīpem (*penny*) dedisses?' In Curia patres singulos nomine salutare solebat; nec libertatem verborum prohibuit. Nam, quum ei orationem habenti dixisset aliquis 'Non intellexi', haec verba **aequo** animo toleravit. In comitiis magistratuum, si filios suos populo commendavit, hoc quoque addidit 'Nolite eos eligere, nisi ipsi **merebuntur**.'

In urbe publice opera multa **exstruxit**, templa deorum alia renovans, alia ornans. Romam igitur dictitabat se latericiam (*made of brick*) invenisse, marmoream relinquere. Civitatem bellis civilibus distractam ad salutem reduxit: provincias **legibus** justis administravit: imperium Romanum longa pace confirmavit. Quas ob res populus eum Patrem Patriae merito titulo nominavit.

XLIV. THE DEFEAT OF VARUS

After a series of campaigns the Romans overran Germany but, just when they thought it conquered, the defeat of Varus in A.D. 9 *lost it to them for ever.*

Praeerat exercitui Romano Quintilius Vārus, nobili familia ortus, vir ingenio **mitis**, **otio** magis quam bello assuetus. Nec Germaniam bene administravit; dictitabat enim oportere barbaros non gladiis domari, sed jure mulceri. Erat inter Chēruscos juvenis nomine Arminius, manu fortis, in-

vīto,[1] -āre, -āvi, -ātum, *avoid, escape* — Fr. *éviter*; Eng. *inevitable*
aequus (adj.), *level, balanced, just, fair, favourable*
mereo,[2] -ēre, -ui, *deserve, win, be deserving* — Eng. *merit*
exstruo,[3] -ere, -struxi, -structum, *build up, build*
lex, lēgis (fem.), *law, condition* — Eng. *legal*

XLIV

mītis (adj.), *gentle, soft, mild*
ōtium, -i (neut.), *leisure*

[1] Note also the compound: *ēvito*, avoid.
[2] Also *mereor*, *-ēri*, *-itus*.
[3] This is a compound of *struo*, build. Note also *construo*, build, **construct**.

Photo Alinari

AUGUSTUS

genio **promptus**, qui consilium rebellionis sēcreto iniit multasque **nationes**, inscio Varo, in societatem adduxit. Is, quum legiones Romanae in **hiberna** reducerentur perque **densissimam** silvam iter facerent, insidias in loco **idoneo** paravit. Quo quum Romani, nihil suspicati, pervenissent, de improviso circumventi se in fugam verterunt. **Impedimentis** relictis, magnoque numero militum occiso, per silvas, per paludes aegre contenderunt. Imbribus continuis ventoque violento conflictati, barbarorum impetum, quoad poterant, vitare sunt conati. Post tres dies alii, spe **amissa**, mortem sua manu obierunt; alii hostium telis sunt trucidati. Ita omnes **fere** perierunt. Vari caput abscissum et hastae praefixum ad Germanorum castra referri Arminius jussit. Hujus cladis nuntios Augustus magno dolore accepit; nec memoriam tantae ignominiae deponere volebat. Nam per continuos menses barbam capillumque submittebat (*let grow*). Caput portis saepe illīdens (*strike against*) vociferabat 'Quintili Vare, legiones mihi redde!' diemque cladis quotannis maestam habebat et lugubrem.

Augusto mortuo, sexto post cladem anno, exercitus Romanus, in Germaniam iterum progressus, ad locum in quo fuerant Vari castra pervenit. Ibi in media silva albentia **ossa**, telorum fragmenta, equorum membra hominumque capita arborum truncis praefixa reppererunt. Dein reliquias suorum maximo luctu **sepeliverunt**.

promptus (part. and adj.), *ready, alert* — Eng. *prompt*
nātio, -iōnis (fem.), *tribe* (usually barbarian) — Eng. *nation*
hīberna, -ōrum (neut.), *winter-quarters*
densus (adj.), *thick, dense*
idōneus (adj.), *suitable, well-fitted, apt*
impedīmentum, -i (neut.), *hindrance, obstacle.* Pl. *baggage, luggage*
āmitto, -ere, -mīsi, -missum, *mislay, lose*
ferē, fermē (adv.), *almost, nearly, roughly speaking*
ōs, ossis (neut.), *bone*
sepelio, -īre, -īvi, sepultum, *bury*

XLV. NERO'S SUICIDE

After many years of misrule Nero was faced by military risings led by generals in the provinces and by the captain of the City Guard. Deserted by all, he committed suicide.

Nuntiata legionum defectione, ad cubiculum Nero se contulit. Media nocte excitatus, e lecto prosiluit, quaerens aliquem cujus manu periret. Deinde, quum neminem reperiret, 'Neque amicum habeo', inquit 'neque inimicum'; procurritque quasi in Tiberim **fluvium** se praecipitaturus. Mutato tamen consilio, quum equum **conscendisset**, comitantibus quattuor amicis, ad villam suburbanam est profectus. Ibi super lectum **vetere** pallio (*cloak*) **stratum** decubuit; mox, litteris a cursore adlatis, cognovit se a senatu hostem esse judicatum. Jamque appropinquabant equites, quibus imperatum est ut eum **vivum** abstraherent. Quos ubi audiit, pugionem, servo adjuvante, ad jugulum **pressit**; et centurioni in cubiculum inrumpenti et auxilium offerenti respondit 'Tu sērius venisti'; tum, voce **deficiente**, inter manus suorum exspiravit.

XLVI. VESPASIAN

Vespasian's habits of industry and talent for organisation set a higher standard of Imperial government than had been seen since the days of Augustus.

Staturā erat quadratā, firmis membris, vultu intento. Valetudine optima utebatur, neque eam **magnopere curavit**.

fluvius, -i (masc.), *river, stream* — Fr. *fleuve*
conscendo,[1] -ere, -di, -sum, *mount, embark*
vetus (adj.), *old, ancient* — Eng. *veteran*
sterno, -ere, strāvi, strātum, *spread, strew, lay out* — Eng. *stratum*
vīvus (adj.), *alive, living*
premo, -ere, pressi, pressum, *press, overcome*
deficio,[2] -ere, -fēci, -fectum, *fail, run short* — Eng. *deficient*

XLVI

magnopere (adv.) (*magno opere*), *greatly, much*
cūro, -āre, -āvi, -ātum, *care for, take care (of), see to* — Eng. *cure*

[1] Compound of *scando*. Cf. *ascendo*, mount, ascend; *descendo*, come down, descend.

[2] Compound of *facio*. Cf. *afficio*, affect; *conficio*, finish off.

Photo Tryde, Copenhagen

VESPASIAN

Membra vero quotidie in sphaeristērio (*games-court*) defricare (*rub down, exercise*) unoque die per singulos menses nihil **edere** solebat. Ordinem vitae hunc tenuit. A prima luce vigilavit; dein, perlectis litteris, amicos admisit; et, dum ab his salutatur, se ipse vestiebat. Luxuriam **conviviorum** contemnebat, ministrosque suos **disciplina** severissima coercebat. Adulescentem quemdam, qui aliquid petiturus intraverat, fragrantem esse unguento **sensit**: tum 'Māluissem', inquit, 'te allium (*garlic*) oboluisse (*smell of*).' Dicacitatis (*talkativeness*) erat plurimae; et sēria jocis saepe intermiscebat. Perseverantia quoque ejus admiratione dignissima videtur: nam **morbo** gravissimo afflictus, **officia** imperatoria non neglegebat; libellos lēgit, legationes audiit cubans. Tum vero, quum se moriturum esse intellegeret, 'Imperatorem', ait, 'stantem mori oportet'; dumque consurgit, inter manus suorum exspiravit.

XLVII. DOMITIAN'S DEATH

Deserting his father's example, Domitian reverted to tyrannical ways; and eventually members of his household conspired to assassinate him.

Primum deliberabant conjurati utrum Domitianum cēnantem an se lavantem aggrederentur sed, ne in tali scelere caperentur, diu quiescebant. Tandem vero Stephanus, unus ex ministris, hoc consilium cepit. Per multos dies, ut suspicionem avertat, manum sinistram, velut **aeger**, lānis (*bandages*) obvolvit; dein, **pugione** sub lanis **celata**, ad

edo, -ere, ēdi, ēsum, *eat* — Eng. *edible*
convīvium, -i (neut.), *feast, banquet* — Eng. *convivial*
disciplīna, -ae (fem.), *teaching, training* — Eng. *discipline*
sentio, -īre, sensi, -sum, *feel, realise, notice* — Fr. *sentir*; Eng. *sensitive*
morbus, -i (masc.), *disease, illness* — Eng. *morbid*
officium, -i (neut.), *duty, service* — Eng. *office*

XLVII

aeger (adj.), *sick, ill, invalid*
pugio, -ōnis (masc.), *dagger, poniard*
cēlo, -āre, -āvi, -ātum, *hide, conceal*

principem intrat, libellum tradit, legentemque pugione confodit. Domitiano tamen non defuit animus. Puerum (qui forte aderat) jubet ministros quam celerrime vocare; dein Stephanum, manibus arreptum, in terram deducit; et pugionem laceratis manibus extorquere conatur. **Saucium** et **paene** morientem aggrediuntur ceteri, inter quos erat quidam e ludo (*school*) gladiatorio; multisque vulneribus luctantem (*struggling*) trucidant. Cadaver ejus feretro (*bier*) populari ex urbe elatum nutrix in villa suburbana sepelivit.

XLVIII. AGRICOLA IN BRITAIN

Agricola by his excellent government did much to civilise the Britons and reconcile them to Roman rule.

Agricola post **consulatum** Britanniae statim praepositus est; et media aestate transgressus provinciam excepit. Ordovicum civitatem prima expeditione **superavit**; dein Monam quoque insulam, multis copiis transvectis, **occupavit.** Quas ob res multae civitates, datis **obsidibus**, arma posuerunt. Sequentibus annis, in Caledoniam progressus, novas **gentes** multas proeliis lacessivit, positisque castellis **coercuit.**

Interea provinciae administrationem nullo modo neglegebat. Nam inter Britannos naturali **prudentia** omnia juste **agebat.** Frumenti ac tributi exactionem mollire instituit;

princeps (adj.), *chief, first*; as noun (masc.), *chieftain*; *Emperor* ENG. *principal*
saucius (adj.), *wounded*
paene (adv.), *almost, nearly* ENG. *pen*insula

XLVIII
consulātus, -ūs (masc.), *consulship, consulate*
supero, -āre, -āvi, -ātum, *overcome, conquer*
occupo, -āre, -āvi, -ātum, *seize, occupy* (*in military sense*)
obses, -idis (comm.), *hostage*
gens, -tis (fem.), *family, race, tribe*
coerceo, -ēre, -ui, -itum, *compel, force, restrain*
prūdentia, -ae (fem.), *foresight, wisdom, prudence*
ago, -ere, egi, actum, *do, perform, drive, lead* ENG. *action*

et ea quae alii legati lucri causa facere solebant, inhonesta arbitrabatur. Sciebat quoque homines incultos quieti et paci per **voluptates** assuescere; postquam igitur bello ac armis eos **satis** tenuerat, commoda pacis ostentare coeperat. Hortabatur enim ut templa, fora, domos exstruerent. Principum filios etiam linguam Romanam **discere** jussit. Mox Britanni porticus et balineas et conviviorum ēlegantiam amare; pecuniam nostram accipere, etiam deos suos nominibus Romanis appellare, sacris nostris uti coeperant. Ii qui nuper sagum (*rough blanket*) brācasque (*breeches*) gesserant, togam induebant. Ita Britannos, ut antea Gallos, longa pax **paulatim** emolliebat.

XLIX*a*. PLINY AND THE CHRISTIANS

Pliny, being appointed by Trajan to a post in Asia Minor, consults his master about the treatment of Christians, whom the Emperors tended to regard as dangerously disloyal.

Soleo, Domine, omnia, de quibus dubito, ad te referre. Quare mihi visum est de Christianis consilium tuum petere. Nuper enim accepi libellum ab indice **ignoto** missum, in quo scripta erant nomina Christianorum nonnullorum. Hos igitur, meo jussu correptos, interrogavi num Christiani essent. Necessarium quoque credidi ex duabus ancillis per tormenta quaerere. Sed nihil aliud **inveni** quam superstitionem pravam. Nam mos est illis, ut affirmant, certo die ante lucem convenire et carmen Christo, quasi deo, dicere; dein sacrāmento se obstringunt ne **furta**, ne latrocinia, ne

voluptas, -ātis (fem.), *pleasure*
satis (adv.), *enough, sufficient*
disco, -ere, didici, *learn* — LAT. *disciplina*
paulātim (adv.), *gradually, bit by bit*

XLIX *a*

ignōtus (adj.), *unknown*
invenio, -īre, -vēni, -ventum, *find, discover, come upon* — ENG. *invention*
furtum, -i (neut.), *theft, deception* — ENG. *furtive*

adulteria committerent. Quo facto discedunt, **rursus**que vespere coeunt, ut cibum communem capiant. Melius **ergo** putavi hoc facere. Omnes, qui accusantur, jussi **imaginem** tuam deorumque simulacra venerari et Christo male dicere. Eis qui pārere volebant, liberavi; eos, qui perseverabant, ad supplicium misi; fuerunt alii, quos, **quia** cives Romani erant, ad urbem remittere constitui. Magnopere vero haesitavi utrum omnes, qui Christiani fuissent, punire debeam an paenitentiae veniam dare. De hac re igitur consilium tuum petere volo.

XLIX*b*. TRAJAN'S ANSWER TO PLINY

Id, quod debuisti, mi Secunde, de Christianis fecisti. Quaerendi non sunt. Si accusantur, sunt puniendi; sed ii, qui negant se Christianos esse et deos nostros venerari volunt, sunt liberandi. Etiam si se olim Christianos fuisse **confitentur**, licet eis **veniam** paenitentia impetrare. Libellus sine nomine **auctoris** propositus auctoritatem non habere debet. Nam pessimum exemplum est neque nostro **saeculo** dignum.

rursus (adv.), *again*
ergo (adv.), *in consequence, therefore*
imāgo, -inis (fem.), *image, statue, ghost*
quia (conj.), *because*

XLIX *b*

confiteor, -ēri, -fessus, *admit, confess*
venia, -ae (fem.), *pardon, permission, leave*
auctor, -ōris (masc.), *author, one responsible*
saeculum, -i (neut.), *age, century, period*

L*a*, *b*. VERRES' MISRULE OF SICILY

Under the Republic the provinces were often the prey of avaricious Roman governors. Verres in Sicily stole works of art and illegally executed Roman citizens. Cicero, in prosecuting him at Rome, gave many examples of his criminal behaviour.

L*a*

Gaius Verres, **furore** incensus, in **forum** oppidi venit. **Ardebant** oculi; toto ex ore crudelitas eminebat; exspectabant omnes quid facturus esset. Tum repente hominem proripi et in foro nudari, virgas parari jussit. Clamabat ille miser se civem Romanum esse. Jubet tamen Verres hominem vehementissime verberari. Inter crepitum plāgarum (*blows*) nulla illius verba audiuntur, nisi haec: CIVIS ROMANUS SUM. Sed, dum nomen civitatis (*citizenship*) implorat, crux homini miserrimo comparatur. O nomen **dulce** libertatis! O jūs nostrae civitatis dulcissimum! In provincia populi Romani homo innocens supplicio indignissimo crudelissimoque periit.

L*b*

Templum Cereris est apud Catinenses, in quo fuit simulacrum deae ipsius **antiquum**. Hoc simulacrum noctu clam Gaii Verris servi ex **sanctissimo** loco sustulerunt. Postero die sacerdotes templi (a feminis enim sacra Cereris confici (*performed*) solebant) rem ad magistratus suos **deferunt**. Omnibus **acerbum**, indignum, luctuosum esse videtur. Tum Verres, populi ira perturbatus, ab se suspicionem sceleris vult removere. Itaque istius jussu servus quidam accusatur; ficti **testes** in eum parantur. Rem totus senatus Catinensium

furor, -ōris (masc.), *madness, fury, rage*
forum, -ī (neut.), *forum, market-place*
ardeo, -ēre, arsi, -sum, *burn* (intrans.), *smoulder* — ENG. *ardent*
dulcis (adj.), *sweet, gentle, pleasant* — FR. *douce*

L*b*

antīquus (adj.), *ancient, old, aged* — ENG. *antique*
sanctus (part. and adj.), *holy, sacred* — ENG. *saint*
dēfero, -ferre, -tuli, -lātum, *report, give* (*a position of command*)
acerbus (adj.), *bitter, sour, harsh*
testis, -is (masc.), *witness* — ENG. *testify*

judicat. Sacerdotes vocantur; ex iis quaeritur secreto in Curia quo modo simulacrum ex templo sit ablatum. Res, quae fuerat jam antea non obscura, sacerdotum testimonio perspicua esse coepit. Servus ille innocens omnium **sententiis** absolvitur.

LI. A ROMAN'S DAY IN TOWN

Like many Romans, Pliny worked hard as a lawyer, besides undertaking official posts at home and in the provinces: social duties, such as witnessing a will or attendance at a 'coming of age' ceremony, helped to make his days very busy.

Diu jam in urbe **haereo.** Si vero interrogas, 'Quid hodie fecisti?', respondebo, 'Officio (*ceremony*) togae virilis interfui; nuptias frequentavi; illius testāmentum signavi, illi consilium dedi.' Haec, quae hodie necessaria esse videntur, **cras inania** fuisse putabo. Si vero plane vīs scire quid faciam, mille **negotiis** conteror. Soleo enim **nonnunquam** in judiciis causas dicere. Ibi ingens turba colligitur; subsellia (*benches*) implentur; nec desunt plausus et laudatio. Sed quae mihi est in talibus rebus delectatio? Hunc laborem relinquere volo. Sed **quiescere** mihi non licet; nam permulti a me postulant ut causas suas mea eloquentia defendam. Vereor ne inertiam meam culpes. Quid ergo faciam? Exemplum tuum imitari constitui. Tu enim obiisti officia, gessisti magistratus; provincias **rexisti**; longo labore otium meruisti. Si ego eodem labore ad eundum **fructum** attinere potero, satis erit.

sententia, -ae (fem.), *feeling, opinion, vote* — Eng. *sentence*

LI

haereo, -ēre, haesi, -sum, *stick, adhere; hesitate* — Eng. *adhesive*
crās (adv.), *to-morrow* — Eng. pro*cras*tinate
inānis (adj.), *empty, useless, vain* — Eng. *inane*
negōtium, -i (neut.), *business, occupation* — Eng. *negotiate*
nonnunquam (adv.), *sometimes*
quiesco, -ere, quiēvi, -ētum, *be quiet, rest*
rego,[1] -ere, rexi, rectum, *rule, govern, direct* — Lat. *rectus*, straight
fructus, -ūs (masc.), *fruit, reward, prize*

[1] Note also the compound: *dirigo*, direct, control.

Boissonas photo

STREET AND TRIUMPHAL ARCH IN ROMAN TOWN OF TIMGAD, NORTH AFRICA

LII. A ROMAN AT HIS COUNTRY-HOUSE

Rich Romans loved to get away from town to the peace of their country estates, where they spent much time in reading and writing as well as in attending to their tenantry.

Quaeris quo modo in Laurentīno (*my Laurentine villa*) diem disponam. Evigilo, cum placuit, plērumque circa horam primam. Clausae **fenestrae** manent. Meditor aliquid; dein, fenestris **apertis**, notarium (*secretary*) voco; et ea, quae **mente** formaveram, dicto. Abit notarius rursusque revocatur rursusque dimittitur. Dein calceos (*shoes*) posco. Vehiculum ascendo, adsumens uxorem vel aliquem amicum. **Peractis** septem milibus passuum, iterum me cubiculo reddo. Paullum redormio; dein **ambulo**; mox orationem Graecam Latinamve clare lego; quod stomachi causa potius quam vocis facere soleo. Ubi hora balinei nuntiata est, in sole ambulo **nudus**, unguor, exerceor (nam saepe pilā ludere placet), denique lavor. Lotus accubo; adponitur cena modesta: lactūcae (*lettuces*), cochleae (*snails*), **ova**, alica (*spelt*) cum mulso (*mead*) et **nive**, olīvae, bētācei (*beetroots*), cucurbitae (*gourds*), bulbi (*onions*), rarius ostrea (*oysters*) vel echīni (*sea-urchins*). Argento puro et antiquo utor. Cenanti mihi liber legitur; post cenam comoedum audio vel lyristen (*lute-player*). Mox cum meis ambulo, quorum in numero sunt **eruditi**. Ita variis sermonibus vespera extenditur. Non tamen omnium dierum eadem est ratio. Interveniunt amici ex proximis oppidis. Datur colonis quoque aliquid temporis. Vēnor **aliquando**; sed non sine pugillaribus (*notebooks*), ut, si apros nullos ceperim, cēras tamen reportem plenas.

fenestra, -ae (fem.), *window, shutters* — Fr. *fenêtre*
aperio, -īre, -ui, apertum, *open, reveal*
mens, -tis (fem.), *mind, intellect* — Eng. *mental*
perago, -ere, -ēgi, -actum, *perform, complete*
ambulo, -āre, -āvi, -ātum, *walk* — Eng. *perambulator*
nūdus (adj.), *naked, bare, unclothed* — Fr. *nu*; Eng. *nude*
ōvum, -i (neut.), *egg* — Fr. *œuf*; Eng. *oval*
nix, nivis (fem.), *snow*
ērudītus (part. and adj.), *polished, learned, well-educated* — Eng. *erudite*
aliquando (adv.), *at some time, at last, at any time*

LIII. ROMAN ENTERTAINMENTS

Public entertainments were popular at Rome, e.g. chariot-racing, fights between wild beasts and gladiators, and dramatic productions, especially of the more spectacular sort.

Scribis te velle scire quid ego in urbe nuper fecerim. Circenses erant; sed hoc genere spectaculi **ne** minime **quidem** delector. Nihil in iis novum, nihil **varium**. Miror igitur quod populus **cupit** currentes equos, homines **curribus** insistentes videre. Pannum (*bit of cloth*)[1] scilicet vulgus vehementi **studio** amat; jam huic colori favent, jam illi. Equos procul noscitant, nomina agitatorum (*drivers*) clamitant; sed in talibus rebus quae delectatio potest esse? Ad ludos quoque nuper ivi, qui (si quaeris) apparatissimi erant. In 'Equo Trojano' multos equites, multos pedites vidi; sed voluptatem nullam hoc spectaculum mihi adfert. Venationes sequuntur, in quibus jam homo invalidus a valentissima bestia vulneratur, jam praeclara bestia vēnābulo (*hunting-spear*) transfigitur; sed **neutrum** mihi placet. **Extremus** dies elephantorum fuit, in quo admiratio magna erat **vulgi**. Me tamen movebat misericordia (*pity*), quum putarem esse quamdam illi belluae cum genere humano **societatem**.

LIV. A ROMAN BOY'S INGENUITY

The sagacity and self-control of Roman boys brought up under the strict discipline of early Republican times is well illustrated by this story.

Mos erat filiis senatorum in Curiam cum **parentibus** intrare. Forte in senatu de re gravissima consultum est; de qua re

ne...quidem (adv.), *not even*
varius (adj.), *changing, different, varied* — Eng. *various*
cupio, -ere, -īvi, -itum, *desire, wish, be eager*
currus, -ūs (masc.), *chariot, carriage*
studium, -i (neut.), *devotion, zeal, study* — Fr. *étude*; Eng. *studious*
neuter (adj.), *neither*
extrēmus (superlative adj.), *last, outside, extreme*
vulgus, -i (neut.), *crowd, mob* — Eng. *vulgar*
societas, -ātis (fem.), *alliance, companionship, kinship* — Fr. *société*; Eng. *society*

LIV

parens, -tis (comm.), *parent*

[1] I.e. the colours worn by the charioteers.

nemini licebat extra Curiam **enuntiare.** Puerum quemdam, nomine Papirium, qui cum patre in Curia fuerat, rogavit mater de qua re senatores illo die consuluissent. Respondit puer sibi non licere id dicere. Tandem vero, urgente matre, mendacio uti constituit. 'Consultum est', inquit, 'utrum oporteat virum unum duas uxores habere an unam feminam duobus viris **nubere.**' Hoc ut mater audivit, magno **pavore** obstupet. Domo **trepidans** egreditur. Ad ceteras matronas rem quam celerrime defert. Postero die pervenit ad Curiam ingens **matronarum** multitudo. Postulant omnes ut una duobus nuberet potius quam uni duae. Senatores ingredientes de hac postulatione **mirantur.** Tum puer Papirius, in medium progressus, totam rem enarrat. Patres prudentiam ejus laudabant; et posthac pueros vetuerunt in Curiam cum parentibus intrare praeter ipsum Papirium.

LV. A ROMAN DUPED BY A GREEK

Greeks, like the Sicilian of this story, were more quick-witted than the average Romans; as the latter sometimes learnt to their cost.

Gaius Canius, eques Romanus, quum Syracusas otii et voluptatis causa se contulisset, dictitabat se **hortos** prope **oram** maritimam emere velle. De qua re certior factus Syracusanus quidam, nomine Pythius, Canium ad cenam invitavit. 'Sunt enim mihi horti', inquit, 'quos tibi **vendere**

ēnuntio, -āre, -āvi, -ātum, *announce, tell fully*
nūbo,[1] -ere, nupsi, -ptum, *marry* (*of the woman*) — Eng. *nuptial*
pavor, -ōris (masc.), *fear, panic, terror*
trepido, -āre, -āvi, -ātum, *be afraid, fear, tremble* — Eng. *intrepid*
mātrōna, -ae (fem.), *married woman, matron*
mīror, -āri, -ātus, *wonder, admire, marvel* (*at*)

LV

hortus, -i (masc.), *garden* — Eng. *horti*culture
ōra, -ae (fem.), *shore, coast*
vendo, -ere, vendidi, venditum, *sell* — Fr. *vendre*

[1] The root is the same as of *nūbes*, cloud, and the literal meaning is 'to put on the veil'.

non possum; sed, si vis, tibi licebit eis, ut tuis, uti.' Promisit Canius se postero die venturum esse. Tum Pythius piscatores multos ad se vocavit et ab eis petiit ut ante hortos suos postero die piscarentur. Ad cenam tempore venit Canius. Convivium a Pythio apparatum laudat; hortorum amoenitatem magnopere approbat. Tum subito ante oculos epulantium (*feasting*) appāret multitudo cymbarum (*boats*). In his piscatores multi, qui magnum numerum **piscium**, quum cepissent, ad oram afferunt et ante pedes Pythii dejiciunt. Dein Canius 'Quaeso', inquit, 'quid est hoc, Pythi? gratissimum est **tot** cymbas, tot pisces videre.' Respondet ille 'Cur mireris? Non enim alio loco majorem copiam piscium invenire possis.' Tum Canius, **cupidine** incensus, a Pythio petit ut hortos sibi vendat. Iterum iterumque petit; tandem impetrat; tantique emit hortos quanti voluit Pythius. Invitat ad hortos postero die amicos suos. Venit ipse māture. Cymbam nullam videt. Quaerit igitur ex proximo **vicino** num feriae (*holiday*) sint piscatorum. Cui roganti respondet alter, 'Nullae feriae sunt, **quoad** scio; sed hic nemo piscari solet. Itaque **heri** mirabar quid **accideret**.'

LVI. A GHOST STORY

A tale recounted by Pliny in a letter to a friend.

Erat Athenis domus magna et spatiosa, ubi per silentium noctis audiri solebat vinculorum **strepitus**; mox apparebat **effigies**, senex promissa **barba** horrentique capillo; qui

piscis, -is (masc.), *fish*
tot (indeclinable adj.), *so many*
cupīdo, -inis (masc.), *desire, longing, greed*
vīcīnus (masc.), *neighbour* (as adj., *neighbouring*) — Eng. *vicinity*
quoad (adv.), *as far as, to the extent that*
heri (adv.), *yesterday* — Fr. *hier*
accido,[1] -ere, -cidi, *befall, happen* — Eng. *accident*

LVI

strepitus, -ūs (masc.), *noise, clatter, clash*
effigies, -ei (fem.), *image, ghost, statue* — Eng. *effigy*
barba, -ae (fem.), *beard* — Fr. *barbe*; Eng. *barber*

[1] This is a compound of *cado*, fall.

manibus **catenas** gerebat quatiebatque. Hanc ob causam deserta est domus; neque quisquam eam emere volebat. Venit Athenas philosophus Athēnodōrus; domum desertam videt; quae sit causa, rogat; tum, totam rem edoctus, parvo pretio emit. Ubi coepit vesperascere (*grow dark, dusk*), in prima parte domūs sedet; **lumen** poscit; servos dimittit; in pugillaribus (*notebook*) aliquid scribit. Non longo post tempore audit vinculorum strepitum. Non oculos tollit; non stīlum (*pen*) remittit. Major fit fragor; jam in **limine**, jam intra limen auditur. Tum respicit ille; videt effigiem senis prope se stantem **digito**que innuentem. Non diu moratus, **surgit** lumenque tollens sequitur. Ibat effigies lento **gradu**: in āream domūs procedit; repente dilapsa Athenodorum deserit. Postero die illum locum effodi jubet. Inveniuntur corpus **aevo** putrefactum et ossa catenis implicita; quae collecta publice sepeliuntur.

LVII. ROME'S DESTINY

Tu regere imperio populos, Romane, **memento,**
Parcere subjectis et debellare superbos.

LVIII. FABIUS SAVED ROME

Unus homo nobis **cunctando** restituit rem;
Non enim rumores ponebat ante salutem.

catēna, -ae (fem.), *chain, bond*
lūmen, -inis (neut.), *light* — Eng. *luminous*
līmen, -inis (neut.), *threshold, doorway*
digitus, -i (masc.), *finger* — Fr. *doigt*; Eng. *digit*
surgo, -ere, surrexi, -rectum, *rise, get up, arise* — Eng. *surge*
gradus, -ūs (masc.), *step, pace* — Eng. *gradual*
aevum, -i (neut.), *age, period*

LVII

memini, -isse, *remember, call to mind* — Eng. *memento* (from the imperative)

LVIII

cunctor, -āri, -ātus, *delay*

LIX. CICERO'S BOAST

O fortunatam, **natam** me consule, Romam!

LX. ANOTHER'S TROUBLE

Suave, mari magno turbantibus **aequora** ventis,
E terra magnum alterius spectare laborem.

LXI. A SPARTAN MOTHER

Mater Lacaena, **clipeo** obarmans filium,
'Cum hoc redi', inquit, 'aut in hoc redi!'

LXII. A WOMAN'S WORD

Crede **ratem** ventis; animum ne crede puellis;
Namque est feminea tutior unda **fide**.

LXIII. FRIENDSHIP

Vincere quum possis, interdum **cede** sodali (*comrade*);
Obsequio quoniam dulces retinentur amici.

LXIV. OPTIMISM

Rebus in adversis animum submittere (*cast down*) noli!
Spem retine; spes una hominem nec morte relinquet.

(nec = not even.)

nascor, -i, nātus, *be born* — Fr. *naître*; Eng. *native*

LX

aequor, -oris (neut.), *flat surface, sea*

LXI

clipeus, -i (masc.), *shield*

LXII

ratis, -is (fem.), *ship, boat, raft*
fides, -ei (fem.), *faith, loyalty, trust*

LXIII

cēdo, -ere, cessi, cessum, *yield, give place, go* — Fr. *céder*; Eng. *cession*

LXV. LOVELY AS A ROSE

Ut rosa **amoena** homini est, quum primo tempore floret,
  Qui me viderunt, his ego amoena fui.

LXVI. LIE LIGHTLY, EARTH

Mollia ne rigidus caespes (*turf*) **tegat** ossa; nec illi,
  Terra, gravis fueris; non fuit illa tibi.

LXVII. FICKLE WOMAN

Nulli se dicit **mulier** mea nubere malle
  Quam mihi, non si se Jupiter ipse petat.
Dicit; sed, mulier **cupido** quod dicit amanti,
  In vento et rapida scribere oportet aqua.

LXVIII. I DO NOT LIKE YOU, Dr FELL

Non amo te, Sabidi; nec possum dicere quare;
  Hoc tantum possum dicere 'non amo te'.

LXIX. AN AUTHOR'S FEARS

Cur non mitto meos tibi, Pontiliane, libellos?
  Ne mihi tu mittas, Pontiliane, tuos.

LXX. LIFE WILL NOT WAIT

Cras te victurum, cras dicis, Postume, **semper**.
  Dic mihi, 'cras' illud, Postume, **quando** venit?

amoenus (adj.), *pleasant, sweet* — Eng. *amenity*

LXVI

mollis (adj.), *soft, gentle, tender*
tego, -ere, texi, tectum, *cover* — Lat. *tectum*, roof, house

LXVII

mulier, -eris (fem.), *woman, wife*
cupidus (adj.), *desirous, eager, longing*

LXX

semper (adv.), *always, for ever*
quando (adv.), (1) interrog. *when?* (2) indef. *at any time* — Fr. *quand?*

LXXI. ROSE AND THORN

Forma bonum fragile est; cito praeterit hora juventae.
  Praeterit et juvenum qui fuit ante decor.
Non semper violae, non semper lilia **florent**:
  Et riget amissa spina relicta rosa.

LXXII. A PRIMITIVE PICNIC

Saepe homines olim prostrati in **gramine** molli
Propter aquae rivum sub **ramis** arboris altae
Non-magnis opibus jucunde corpora habebant,
Praesertim quum tempestas **ridebat** et anni
Tempora **pingebant** viridantes floribus herbas.

LXXIII. MASTER OF HIS SOUL

Regem non faciunt **opes**,
Non vestis Tyriae color,
Non auro nitidae fores.
Rex est qui **metuit** nihil;
Rex est qui cupiit nihil.
Hoc regnum sibi quisque dat.

LXXIV. DOOMSDAY

Omnia mors poscit. Lex est, non poena perire;
  Hic aliquo **mundus** tempore nullus erit.

flōreo, -ēre, -ui, *flower, flourish*

LXXII

grāmen, -inis (neut.), *grass*
rāmus, -i (masc.), *branch*
rīdeo, -ēre, rīsi, rīsum, *laugh, smile* — Eng. *deride*
pingo, -ere, pinxi, pictum, *paint* — Eng. *picture*

LXXIII

opes, -um (fem.), *wealth, power, resources*
metuo, -ere, -ui, *fear, be afraid of*

LXXIV

mundus, -i (masc.), *world, universe* — Fr. *monde*

LXXV. FAREWELL, MY SOUL!

Animula vagula blandula,
Hospes comesque corporis,
Quae nunc abibis in loca?
Pallidula, rigida, nudula.
Nec, ut soles, dabis **jocos.**

jocus, -i (masc.), *jest, joke*

Note. *animula* is diminutive of *anima*, soul; *vagulus* of *vagus*, wandering; *blandulus* of *blandus*, fond; *pallidulus* of *pallidus*, pale; *nudulus* of *nudus*, naked.

EXERCISES

A NOTE ON WORD-ORDER

The word-order in a Latin sentence is very different from the word-order in an English sentence. There is no hard and fast rule; but generally the Verb will come last in a sentence. Usually therefore

(1) Both *subject* and *object* precede the verb:

e.g. The boy *heard* the wolf. Puer lupum *audivit.*

(2) All the *circumstances* under which an action takes place (i.e. time, cause, purpose, manner, etc.) precede the main verb which describes the action:

e.g. The boy fled with great haste when he heard the wolf at nightfall.
Vespere lupo audito puer summa celeritate fugit.
(TIME) (CAUSE) (MANNER) (ACTION).

(3) Subordinate clauses, describing cause, purpose, etc., precede the main verb:

e.g. The boy came to the city to see the girl secretly.
Puer, ut puellam clam videret, ad urbem venit.

Note that in the purpose-clause itself, too, the object (*puellam*) and the adverb of manner (*clam*) precede the verb (*videret*).

I–V AND SUPPLEMENTARY A. RELATIVE CLAUSES

In a Relative Clause (e.g. the woman *whom they praise*),

(1) the VERB goes normally in the INDICATIVE;
(2) the RELATIVE PRONOUN (who = *qui, quae, quod*, etc.)

takes its *gender* and *number* from its antecedent, here 'woman', i.e. *feminine singular*:

takes its *case* from the relative verb, here *accusative*, object of 'praise':

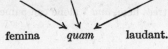

femina *quam* laudant.

I

1. I am-looking-for the man who has taken Helen.
2. That woman, whom you see, does not love her husband.
3. They went to Troy, which is across the sea.
4. Who will praise the plan which Paris has made?
5. Priam, whose name you have heard, is this man's father.
6. (Those) who are bold receive the greatest praise.

II

In English the Relative Pronoun is often left out: in Latin it must be expressed.

1. The Trojan * you had been praising suddenly seized Helen.
2. Greeks defeated Trojans in the war * Homer writes about.
3. The spear * he threw pierced Hector's body.
4. The Greek * you are-afraid-of is Achilles.
5. The sailors * here-present will prepare the ship.
6. Is the man * now going-forward your son?

III

1. He will lose the wife he has abandoned.
2. (He) who cannot see wanders from the road.
3. They explored the city they had left.
4. Aeneas called by name the woman he was looking-for.
5. The old man he is carrying on his shoulders is his father.
6. I took the hand of his son, who is called Ascanius.

IV

If the same person or thing is referred to in two main clauses, Latin sometimes joins the clauses with a relative pronoun, where English has 'and' with a demonstrative:

e.g. I sent him a book *and* he read *it*.
Librum ei misi, *quem* legit.

1. Two boys were born to (*ex*) his brother's daughter, *and* Amulius wished to kill *them*.
2. He put the boys in the river, *and* presently a shepherd found *them*.
3. She went to her brother *and* asked *him* many things.
4. The she-wolf fed on milk the two boys she had found.
5. The shepherd took them to his wife, *and she* brought them up at home.
6. There are many trees here, *and* I alone can name *them*.

V

1. Bring me the rake with which you killed Remus.
2. They both wanted to rule the city which had been founded.
3. Romulus saw twelve birds, *and* the people therefore gave *him* the kingdom.
4. Remus was-contemptuous-of the walls they had built.
5. We founded a city *and* I gave my name *to it*.
6. He alone now held the kingdom which his brother also had sought.

In addition to the relative pronoun, the following relative adverbs are important: *quo*, whither; *unde*, whence, from where; *ubi*, where or when; *quomodo* and *quemadmodum*, in the way in which, as; *ut*, as:

e.g. Troia urbs est quo Paris navigat.
Troy is the city to which (whither) Paris is sailing.

[Relative pronouns, other than *qui*, are *quantus*, as much as, as large as; *qualis*, of the sort that; *quot*, as many as.]

1. There was in Asia a large city, *from which* Paris came.
2. Aeneas is making for the gate of the city, *to which* (whither) his son has already gone.
3. Let Remus seek an omen, *as* his brother Romulus has sought (one).
4. Amulius put the two boys into the river, *where* a wolf saw them.
5. *When* Paris had made his plan, he was silent about it.
6. Helen went to the ship alone, *as* she had been bidden.

VI–XIII*b*. PARTICIPLES

The Ablative Absolute

In Latin, PARTICIPLES are more frequently used than in English. Thus, 'a city *was founded and* he did as follows' would be 'a city *having been founded*, he did as follows'. Here the founding of the city is the *circumstance*[1] which preceded the doing of what followed. So 'city' will be put in the *Ablative* and the past participle passive ('having been founded') will agree with it:

e.g. Urbe condita, haec fecit.

N.B. This Ablative (known as the Ablative Absolute) will usually come *at the beginning of the sentence.*

VI

1. His brother having-been-killed, Romulus founded the city.
2. These things having-been-done, he invited the neighbours into the state.
3. A hundred citizens having-been-chosen, he did everything with these men's advice.
4. These maidens having-been-seized, the Romans now had wives.
5. The enemy having-been-conquered, you will receive no more injuries.
6. Romulus not having-been-found, they chose another king.

[1] Cf. Ex. XXVI.

VII

English verbs possess an active past participle (e.g. 'having taken') as well as a passive past participle (e.g. 'having been taken'). Latin verbs (with the exception of deponents; see Ex. x) possess a PASSIVE PAST PARTICIPLE ONLY (e.g. *instructus*, having been drawn up). '*Having drawn up* the army, Arruns approached' must therefore be converted into:

The army *having been drawn up*, Arruns approached.
Acie *instructa*, Arruns appropinquavit.

1. Having made-ready their army, the enemy began a battle.
2. Having recognised his face, Arruns rushed at Brutus.
3. The kings being driven from the city, the Romans wanted to have consuls.
4. Having drawn up the cavalry, the king waited-for the legions.
5. Having thrown one spear, he asked for another.
6. Paris made-for Troy after-seizing (Participle) Helen.

VIII

All Latin verbs (including deponents) possess an ACTIVE PRESENT PARTICIPLE (e.g. *nuntians*, announcing; *conans*, trying). Such a present participle should only be used when its action (i.e. announcing, trying, etc.) takes place *at the same time* as the action of the main verb:

e.g. The Etruscans shouting (= while the Etruscans were shouting) Cocles waited.
Etruscis clamantibus, Cocles exspectabat.

N.B. *Sum* (I am) possesses no present participle. Sometimes therefore an Ablative Absolute is made up of a noun and an adjective or of two nouns, e.g. Horatius (being) our leader = Horatio duce.

1. Others being afraid, Horatius alone was bold.
2. The enemy trying to dislodge him, Horatius stood unmoved.
3. *In-the-hearing-of* (Participle) the Etruscans, we raised another shout.
4. The Romans were breaking the bridge (*while*) Horatius *held up* (Participle) the attack.
5. The city (being) safe, he swam across the Tiber.
6. (*While*) the king *followed* (Participle), his brother led the line-of-march.

IX*a*

A Latin participial clause may often be equivalent to a dependent clause in English, e.g. 'castris munitis' may stand for 'when the camp had been fortified'. In this exercise, substitute *past* participles for English dependent clauses.

1. When a great uproar was made, the nobles were frightened.
2. Since the people were moved with anger, a secession was made.
3. After they had left the city, the people made this plan.
4. When they had fortified the camp, they waited for many days.
5. As Agrippa has been sent, we are willing to hear your plans.
6. After hearing his words they decide to accept the terms.

IX*b*

In this exercise, substitute *present* participles for English dependent clauses.

1. Since its members were unwilling to feed it, the body was sick.
2. While Agrippa was speaking, it pleased the people to be-silent.
3. While we were bringing help, the enemy were leading out their forces.
4. As the messengers arrived, the soldiers raised a shout.
5. With the tribunes helping, we can destroy the Patricians.
6. Let us accept this counsel, since disagreement is arising among our leaders.

X

The past participle of a Deponent Verb is ACTIVE in meaning, e.g. *questus* = having complained (from *queror*); *usus* (from *utor*) = having used.

Try to find deponent verbs to express the active past participles in the following sentences.

1. Since Verginia had complained about Appius, her father was angry.
2. Since Appius had tried to lead off the girl, the mob began to complain.
3. After her father went forward, the married women all wept.
4. When his daughter followed, Verginius seized a knife.
5. The consul having spoken, they began the battle.
6. When a storm arose, they all returned to camp.

XI

1. When they heard this, they all praised his courage.
2. Summer was approaching and he had not put on his toga.
3. Few people complained when Cincinnatus had been made dictator.
4. He left the ditch he was digging and greeted the ambassadors.
5. Suddenly, wiping off the sweat, the dictator asked-for his toga.
6. If our courage is destroyed, how shall the city be safe?

XII

1. Coriolanus was setting out for Rome, and the senators were afraid.
2. Our children will shed no more tears when the city has been saved.
3. Now that power is given you, bring help to the city.
4. Accept my advice and return whence you set out.
5. Having heard these words, he refused to go forward.
6. On his mother's persuasion, he returned home.

XIII *a*

1. As the Gauls approached, some of us fled, others remained.
2. When they had killed the old men, the Gauls plundered the houses.
3. Now that the army is defeated, I will await death.
4. After the children had been carried to the citadel, the old men returned home.
5. As Papirius was sitting there, his wife was preparing the fire.
6. Though the rest were frightened, the boldest advanced to the Forum.

XIII *b*

'Clade nuntiata, agros petebant' might be translated

(*a*) After the defeat was announced, they made for the fields,
(*b*) They made for the fields when the defeat had been announced,
(*c*) The defeat was announced and then they made for the fields,
and in various other ways.

Translate the following sentences, using in each instance a different way of expressing the participial clause.

1. Armis raptis, Manlius hostium ducem trucidavit.
2. Gallis arcem ascendentibus, anseres excitati sunt.
3. His donis acceptis, omnes urbem reliquerunt.
4. Tempestate orta, Capitolium ascendere non conati sunt.
5. Magno clangore facto, querebantur Galli.
6. Flentibus ceteris, senes virtutem servaverunt.

XIV*a*–XVII. INDIRECT STATEMENT

XIV*a*

An Indirect Statement (e.g. they say *that the enemy is preparing an ambush*) may be introduced not merely by a verb of saying, but also by such verbs as 'think', 'know', 'believe', 'hear', 'hope'. In Latin, (1) the verb of an Indirect Statement is in the INFINITIVE, (2) its subject is in the ACCUSATIVE:

e.g. Dicunt *hostes* insidias *parare.*

N.B. Use *se* (acc.) = 'him himself' (or 'they themselves') when this pronoun refers to the *same person as the subject of the main verb*:[1]

e.g. Putat *se* fortem esse.
He thinks *he* (himself) is brave.

1. Having accepted these terms, they say *that* they are losing all hope.
2. We hear *that* there is a pass above the plain.
3. 'I know', said[2] the Roman, '*that* we shall all be miserable.'
4. These soldiers say *that* they are ready and *that* the others are coming.
5. He tells me *that* the journey is long.
6. Since the Samnites are following, we know *that* danger is at hand.

XIV*b*

In an Indirect Statement the speaker may be referring to an event

(1) which, *at the time of his speaking*, is *about to* happen (*Future Infinitive*),

(2) which *is* happening *as he speaks* (*Present Infinitive*),

(3) which *has* happened *before he speaks* (*Perfect Infinitive*):

e.g. He says	he will come.	Dicit se	venturum esse.
	he is coming.		venire.
	he has come.		venisse.
He said	he would come.	Dixit se	venturum esse.
	he was coming.		venire.
	he had come.		venisse.

1. They believed the soldiers had surrendered their arms.
2. He said the Romans would all be put-in-chains.
3. I did not say that I accepted these terms.
4. He again said he was sending the generals back to the enemy.
5. When the soldiers came in, we knew that we had been defeated.
6. Do you think the shops will be shut?

[1] For third person only.
[2] *ait* or *inquit* should be used with Direct Speech for 'says he', 'said he'.

XV

Often, in English, an Indirect Statement is expressed by a plain Infinitive, especially after verbs of *promising* (*promitto*, *polliceor*), *hoping* (*spero*), and *threatening* (*minor*). Usually this refers to a future event (e.g. I hope *to come* = spero *me venturum esse*), though occasionally to a present (e.g. I believe him *to be* evil = credo eum malum *esse*).

In Latin, the Accusative (e.g. *me*, *eum*) must *never* be omitted.

1. Pyrrhus hoped to bribe Fabricius.
2. But he answered that he was not a bad man.
3. The king promised to send him many presents.
4. He thought a (wild) beast would frighten him.
5. Fabricius however showed he was not frightened by an elephant.
6. 'Why', said Gaius, 'do you not threaten to kill me to-day?'

XVI

Latin never uses *dico* followed by *non*, but always *nego*, I deny:

e.g. He *said* the serpent had *not* got feet.
Negavit serpentem pedes habere.

1. They say this dragon does not see us.
2. He promised to kill the beast with his artillery.
3. Regulus will have learnt that the soldiers are in great danger.
4. The general said that the army would not turn in flight.
5. Do you know that the camp has been pitched not far from the river?
6. We believe that this disgraceful beast will be overcome by such a plan.

XVII

1. Regulus promised the Carthaginians that he would return.
2. Did you say you wouldn't stay in prison?
3. He persuaded them that such a peace was bad.
4. The wretched man thought his friends would not receive him.
5. They said that, when Regulus had been killed, they would not carry-on the war.
6. I know it is disgraceful to stay in the city.

XVIII–XXIV. MIXED PARTICIPLES

XVIII

Revisionary Exercise—Ablative Absolute

1. When the sun rises, the mountains will be seen.
2. Under the leadership of Flaminius, the Romans came near to the lake.
3. The clouds were dispersed and the light of the sun returned.
4. As the first hour was approaching, they made-ready their arms.
5. He gave the signal and promised we would win.
6. When Pomponius spoke, we knew that many Romans had been killed.

XIX

'Pomponius having arisen from his seat said many things.' Here 'Pomponius' is the *subject* of the main verb 'said', as well as of the participle 'having arisen'. It must therefore go into the Nominative, and the participle 'having arisen' will agree with it:

Pomponius, ex sede ortus, multa dixit.

1. The magistrate went forward and announced that we had been defeated.
2. Fabius was made dictator and strengthened the city's defences.
3. The walls being strengthened, we defended the town.
4. Flaminius, as he died, said he had not lacked courage.
5. Having dallied in the mountains he at last advanced.
6. Few men, when sent to prison, think they are happy.

XX

'Pomponius having arisen from his seat, we praised him.' Here 'Pomponius' is the *object* of the main verb 'praised' and will go in the Accusative:

Pomponium ex sede ortum laudavimus.

1. He said he would take the city and burn (it).
2. Having summoned a herald, he bade (him) announce these things.
3. Why, when you had led out the infantry, did you desert (them)?
4. They sent fresh troops to Spain and did not recall (them).
5. When he had brought back the army, he realised that (it) had lost all hope.
6. They say that Hannibal rode up to the city and threw a spear over the walls.

XXI

An English sentence which contains a past participle *active* has to be re-cast in order to allow the use of a Latin past participle *passive* (cf. Ex. VII). In making such a change, enquire carefully whether the participle may refer to the *subject* or *object* of the main verb.

1. Four horsemen were sent to Hannibal but did not reach him.
2. We hear that the Romans have cut off Hasdrubal's head and thrown it into his brother's camp.
3. When he learnt of Hasdrubal's arrival, he marched to the other consul's camp.
4. The foragers rode fast and captured the letters that had been sent.
5. Seeing his brother's head Hannibal knew he could not capture Rome.
6. The enemy were drawn up in line and attacked us on the flank.

XXII

In each of the following sentences a participial clause must be used. If the noun of the participial clause turns out to be also the *subject* (or *object*) of the main verb, then that noun will be in the *Nominative* (or *Accusative*). *Otherwise* the noun and its participle will be put in the *Ablative Absolute*.

1. Hannibal was fleeing from the enemy and the old man received him as a guest.
2. Now that the ambassador has been seen, I shall not try to escape him.
3. I have been received as a guest, but am not safe in Prusias' house.
4. The king had decided to betray him and hand him over to the Romans.
5. When death is expected we fear it less.
6. Nero read the despatch and realised the danger was great.

XXIII

Re-construct the following sentences so that they contain a participle.

1. Scipio deis gratias egit et promisit se iterum acturum esse.
2. Magno favore fruitus est sed non odium inimicorum evitare potuit.
3. Rostra ascendit et haec locutus est.
4. Quamquam pudore victus est, non tamen auxilium poposcit.
5. Bellum feliciter gessi: non igitur accusari debeo.
6. Hunc nebulonem in Foro relinquamus et in Capitolium eamus.

XXIV

1. They say that a serpent was brought and drove away the plague.
2. Shall we not make a journey and summon Aesculapius?
3. I hear they entered the temple on the invitation of the inhabitants.
4. I think, when we have put out food, the serpent will take it.
5. Do you realise that it[1] was not carried to the island but swam across itself?
6. The priests themselves sought help with-a-view-to-saving[2] the state.

XXV–XXVI*b* AND SUPPLEMENTARY B, C

XXV

The Accusative Case is used to denote:

1. The *extent* of an action
   (*a*) in regard to *time*:

   e.g. *Tres horas* ambulavi.
   I walked *for three hours.*

   (*b*) in regard to *space*:

   e.g. *Tria milia* passuum ambulavi.
   I walked *three miles.*

2. The *goal* of an action:

   e.g. *ad urbem* (to the city)
   or *in urbem* (into the city) veni.

(Note that prepositions are here added to clarify the sense.)

1. Men are saying that Flaminius has gone to Greece.
2. He promises that their cities shall be free for many years.
3. The herald repeated these words and came to the city.
4. They followed him for three miles and then returned home.
5. The Greeks, filled with joy, shouted for two hours.
6. I think the Isthmus is about five miles broad.

[1] Should agree with *anguis* in *gender.*
[2] Future participle.

The Ablative Case is used to express three ideas.

1. *Origin* of an action, e.g. *Romulo* natus = born of Romulus' lineage. This idea extends also to (*a*) the *agent* of an action, e.g. *a Romulo* occisus est = he was killed by Romulus; (*b*) the *place from which*, e.g. *ab urbe* proficiscitur = he sets out from the city.

1. Summoned by his master the bailiff came from the fields.
2. After speaking an hour, he drove the man from the senate.
3. This man thinks he knows more than-his-master.[1]
4. When bidden by Cato, get up from bed.

2. The *circumstances*[2] of an action, expressing the idea of

(*a*) *Accompaniment: cum patre* ivit = he went with his father.

N.B. With personal pronouns *cum* follows instead of preceding: *mecum, secum, vobiscum*, etc.

(*b*) *Manner: magna difficultate* locutus est = he spoke with great difficulty (sometimes with *cum*, especially when there is no qualifying adjective).

5. Do you think Cato ruled his slaves with too much harshness?
6. With real pleasure he enjoyed[2] the same food as they used.
7. He did not neglect eloquence and talked often with his friends.
8. Getting up from his seat he spoke with great authority.

3. (*a*) *Place at which* action takes place: e.g. *in urbe*[3] manet = he is remaining in the city.

(*b*) *Time at which*: e.g. *tertia hora* = at the third hour (no preposition).

9. He was accused in the law-courts and himself accused many.
10. In endurance of danger he surpassed other Romans.
11. In the houses of the nobles luxury was excessive.
12. In the evening he studied the books he had bought.

Supplementary B

'Place to which', 'Place at which', 'Place from which' must be treated somewhat differently with the NAMES of Towns and Small Islands; also the words *domus*, home, *rus*, country, and *humus*, ground.

1. *Place to which.* No preposition is used, e.g. *Romam* venio; *domum* redeo, etc.

[1] The Ablative of Comparison expresses the measuring point from which the comparison is made, e.g. *Gaio* Marcus altior est, lit. Starting from Gaius, Marcus is taller; Marcus is taller than Gaius.

[2] A few deponent verbs are constructed with an Ablative of this sort, e.g. *hoc ludo* fruor, I enjoy this game, lit. I enjoy myself with this game.

[3] For the Locative Case, see below.

2. *Place at which.* No preposition:

(*a*) In names of the *first or second declensions singular* a special case (the Locative) is used, equivalent to the Genitive, e.g. *Corinthi*, at Corinth (Corinthus); *domi*, at home.

(*b*) *Otherwise*[1], the Locative is equivalent to the plain Ablative, e.g. *Athenis*, at Athens (Athenae); *rure*, in the country.

3. *Place from which.* Plain Ablative, with no preposition, e.g. Roma venit = He comes from Rome.

1. Do they use the Greek language at Athens?
2. He was born at Gades but went to Rome.
3. Having delayed at Heraclea, he started out in the evening.
4. At that time Dido was queen in Carthage.
5. The woman you have sent for has come from Corinth.
6. They say at Locri that their customs are good.

SUPPLEMENTARY C

Value is expressed in two ways:

(*a*) General value: by *Genitive*:[2] e.g. *magni* est = it is of great value.

(*b*) Particular (i.e. money) value: by *Ablative*: e.g. hoc *tribus sestertiis* emo = I buy this for three sesterces.

The principal money values in which the Romans reckoned were:

1. The sesterce, *sestertius, -i* (masc.), about $2\frac{1}{2}d.$
2. The talent, *talentum, -i* (neut.), about £240.

The most usual verbs are: *aestimo* (XXVI *a*), value, think worth; *emo* (XXVI *b*), buy; *vendo*, sell.

1. My bailiff had bought ten birds for eighty sesterces.
2. Cato valued abstinence more than other virtues.
3. This book you bought for twenty sesterces I myself think worth very little.
4. He valued the house highly but sold it for two talents.

[1] That is, in names of the first or second declensions plural, or of the third declension.

[2] Generally the Genitive Singular neuter of an adjective, e.g. *tanti*, at so much; *parvi*, at a little; *minoris*, less; etc.

XXVII–XXIX. FINAL CLAUSES

A Final or 'Purpose' Clause is introduced by *ut*, 'in order that', or *ne*, 'in order that not', 'lest'. Its verb will be in the Subjunctive. If the main verb of the sentence is PRIMARY, i.e. *present*, or *future*, or *perfect* (='I have done'), then the verb of the Final Clause will be *Present Subjunctive*:

e.g. The citizens are making all preparations, *with the intention of* defending the city.
Cives, ut urbem defendant, omnia parant.

XXVII

Phrases denoting purpose are printed in italics and should be translated by *ut* (or *ne*) with the Subjunctive.

1. The Romans at once send ambassadors to Carthage *to offer* the citizens terms of peace.
2. We believe that they have been getting-together bronze, *in order that they may not be-without* weapons.
3. The Carthaginians have fortified the walls *so that* the Romans *may not enter* the city.
4. The Romans do not spare the children, *for-fear-of being-without* bread themselves.
5. A few say they will surrender the city *rather than be carried off* to enslavement.
6. The soldiers are allowed to buy slaves *for the purpose of carrying* home their silver and gold.

XXVIII

When the main verb is HISTORIC (i.e. *imperfect*, or *perfect* (='I did') or *pluperfect*), then the verb of the Final Clause will be *Imperfect Subjunctive.*

1. He consulted his friends *in order that he might answer* the Roman envoy.
2. Antiochus finally accepted the terms *so as to have* the Roman people's friendship.
3. The king did not march to Alexandria *for fear lest* Popilius *might forbid* (it).
4. *To understand* the Roman character, you ought to keep Popilius' words in mind.
5. 'I carried out your orders', said he, '*on purpose to show* you that I was not using trickery.'
6. The ambassador had set out for Syria *to give* the king a letter.

XXIX

In a Final Clause, 'in order that no-one' is *ne quis*; 'in order that never'; *ne quando*, etc., not *ut* followed by a negative pronoun or adverb.

1. A Gallic deserter entered and implored that the consul might spare him.
2. But Quintius immediately killed him so that his wife might enjoy a novel spectacle.
3. I tell you these things in case you should think the Romans were always noble.
4. 'I will draw my sword', said he, 'and pierce him through so that no one may save him.'
5. Roman generals often employed violence to prevent anyone from refusing to obey them.
6. They believed that they ought to use great harshness for fear danger might be at hand.

XXX–XXXII. INDIRECT COMMANDS

In an Indirect Command (e.g. 'I ordered him *to go*' or 'I ordered him *not to go*') the idea of purpose or prevention is clearly present. So the same construction is used as in Finals: i.e. *ut* or *ne* with Present or Imperfect Subjunctive.

Verbs which introduce such indirect commands are *impero*, 'order' and *suadeo*, 'advise', which take the Dative; *hortor*, 'exhort' and *moneo*, 'warn', which take the Accusative.

XXX

1. Gracchus, who was tribune, urged the people to scorn omens and with him to save the state.
2. Ten years before, his brother had tried to persuade the nobles to give up their lands.
3. An enormous crowd warned him not to rouse the anger of the senators by overmuch pride.
4. Gracchus was declared an enemy and Nasica set out to pursue him.
5. The consul ought to have begged his soldiers to avoid excessive slaughter.
6. He had ordered the tribune Octavius not to resist the plans he had made.

XXXI

Jubeo, 'command', is always followed by an Infinitive, as also is *veto*, 'forbid'; and 'I *command* you *not* to go, etc.' must always be translated by '*veto* te ire', *jubeo* never being followed by a negative.

1. 'I am sure', said he 'that we ought not any longer to put up with the arrogance of the nobles.'
2. Recently the magistrate forbade us to use the baths, so that the consul's wife might use them.
3. Some people still delaying there, the consul gave orders that this magistrate should be punished.
4. He urged us vigorously to discover the man and bring him back to him.
5. We have been told lately not to entrust ourselves to the nobles, who have such great pride and audacity.
6. Why, for so slight a reason, did he order that poor yokel to be beaten to death?

XXXII

'I persuade', 'I warn', etc. may be followed either by (*a*) *a command*: e.g. I persuade you *to* go = tibi persuadeo ut eas, or (*b*) *a statement*: e.g. I persuade you *that* this is true = tibi persuadeo hoc verum esse.

1. At first, when the Romans asked for battle, Marius forbade them to leave the camp.
2. The Teutons warned him that they were going to make straight for Italy.
3. The enemy are persuaded that they have an opportunity which we know they have not got.
4. Many of the soldiers told Marius that they were in need of water.
5. He urged them to defeat the enemy and buy the water with their blood.
6. 'Our general advises us', say they, 'not to use javelins to-day but to use swords and shields.'

XXXIII–XXXV

Revision: Finals and Indirect Commands

XXXIII

Sometimes a noun or pronoun contained in a Final Clause appears in the main clause also: e.g. 'I sent *soldiers* in order that *they* might kill Marius.'

In such an instance *ut* may be replaced by the relative *qui*, which will (as any ordinary relative) take its gender and number from its antecedent, and its case from its relation to the verb of its clause.

1. The magistrate sent a soldier to Minturnae to find Marius and murder him.
2. This soldier brought a sword wherewith to kill him.
3. With bold words the general frightened the man who had been sent to perform this task.
4. After a short space, his freedom restored, Marius obtained a ship on which he might escape to Africa.
5. Tell me a Roman whom I may call a greater general than Marius.
6. When the Teutons were conquered he returned to Rome, but he was a better consul in war than in peace.

XXXIV *a*

1. On entering the city, Sulla gave orders that his enemies should not escape.
2. He made a speech whereby to persuade the senators not to alter his plans.
3. Spoils were taken from those who were killed and given to those who had killed (them).
4. The dictator is publishing lists whereby men may know that presently they will be murdered.
5. A senator was sent to beg Sulla to make an end of these punishments.
6. After doing these things, he tried to restore to the nobles the power which Gaius Gracchus had taken from them.

XXXIV *b*

When a Final Clause contains a *comparative* adjective or adverb, *ut* is replaced by *quo*:

e.g. I tell you this in order that you may understand the language *better*.
Hoc tibi dico *quo melius* linguam intellegas.

1. I suppose he used violence to overcome his enemies more easily.
2. To make the punishments more cruel, they dug out men's eyes and cut out their tongues.
3. He has gone right up to those lists, the more easily to read the names which are written on them.
4. The slaves showed where their master was hiding, *as-they-hoped-to* win (Final) greater rewards.
5. *He-wanted-no-one-to* recognise his face; (so) he used to wander through the streets in the dark.
6. As soon as he saw the street was broader, he turned back home, *to avoid* meeting his enemies.

XXXV

Re-write the following sentences in Latin, with a variation on the construction here used.

1. Collem ascenderant *ut* facilius hostes spectarent.
2. *Ei impera ne* sacerdotibus *parcat.*
3. Copias adduxit multas *ut* oppidum Judaeorum expugnaret.
4. Vaccam tibi mitto *ut ea* in sacrificium utaris.
5. Pompeius *milites* aggerem *facere iussit.*
6. Huc adveni *ut* candelabrum aureum comiti tuo donem.

XXXVI–XXXVIII. INDIRECT QUESTIONS

An Indirect Question (I ask *what you are doing*) may be introduced by such verbs as 'ask', 'tell', 'know', 'hear', 'wonder', etc.

A. The verb of an Indirect Question goes in the *subjunctive.*

B. Its tense will vary according as the questioner is referring to an action which

(1) *is about to* take place: I ask what you will do;
(2) *is* taking place at the time of speaking: I ask what you are doing;
(3) *has* already taken place: I ask what you have done (or did).

If the main verb (of 'asking', etc.) is *primary,* then the indirect verb will be

(1) future subjunctive: rogo quid facturus sis;
(2) present subjunctive: rogo quid facias;
(3) perfect subjunctive: rogo quid feceris.

An Indirect Question may be introduced by *quis, quid* (who, what); *cur* (why); *quo modo* (how); *quam* + adj. (how), e.g. *quam fortis,* how brave; *quo* (whither); *unde* (whence); *ubi* (where); *quando* (when); etc.

XXXVI

1. 'My friends', said he, 'have asked me what I have in mind.'
2. They want to know how I will act when I have collected soldiers.
3. Meanwhile I will tell you why I have already done all this unarmed.
4. Catiline shows us in what great danger the Senate House stands.
5. (Those) who are-on-the-watch will learn with how great a blaze the city can be destroyed.
6. They went as if about to greet Cicero, so that they might more easily kill him.

XXXVII

If the main verb (of 'asking', etc.) is *historic*, then the verb of the Indirect Question goes into a *historic tense* of the Subjunctive.

e.g. I asked what you { would do (i.e. after I spoke).
were doing (i.e. as I spoke).
had done (i.e. before I spoke).

Rogavi quid tu { facturus esses.
faceres.
fecisses.

1. Milo did not know when his wife would set out with him.
2. Did you tell me that he knew what Clodius had schemed?
3. I know he was totally ignorant where the man had gone to.
4. The magistrates, summoning Milo's slaves, asked them how the Senate House had been burned.
5. The crowd replied that they had been cremating Clodius's body and that by accident the Senate House had been burned too.
6. Cicero discovered how difficult it was to show that Milo had not killed Clodius.

XXXVIII

(1) When an Indirect Question expects a *plain* answer, 'yes' or 'no', it is introduced by *num* (not by *nonne*):

e.g. I ask *whether* (or *if*) you have done this.
Rogo *num* hoc feceris.

(2) When an Indirect Question expects a choice between two *alternative* answers, it is introduced by *utrum*...*an*:

e.g. I do not know *whether* this happened by chance *or* by design.
Nescio *utrum* hoc casu *an* consilio acciderit.

N.B. 'Whether...*or not*' is 'utrum...*necne*'.

1. You will perhaps ask whether Caesar showed great courage in his youth.
2. Caesar said the pirates did not know what value the Romans set on him.
3. (Those) who had captured him were uncertain whether he was laughing at them or not.
4. He collected (some) armed men and told them where the pirates had come from.
5. For he had promised that, when he was released, he would bring men to take vengeance on them.
6. I am asking whether you all know whether Miletus is an island or a city.

XXXIX*a*

Answer the following questions in Latin. In each answer, include a *main verb* and introduce *at least one* of the constructions dealt with in this book.

1. Quos deos venerabantur Britanni?
2. Cur in Britanniam transierant Galli quidam?
3. Cur hi Galli in Britannia permanserunt?
4. Quomodo vivebant plerique Britannorum?
5. Quomodo natio Gallorum sacrificia faciebat?

XXXIX*b*

Draw a map of Britain as the Romans imagined it to be.

XXXIX*c*

From the vocabulary of this piece, and using the subject-matter if required (e.g. an Indirect Statement: Dico milites novo genere pugnae territos esse = I say that the soldiers were frightened by a new kind of fighting), compose sentences in Latin to illustrate:

1. An Indirect Command.
2. An Indirect Statement.
3. A Participle in the Accusative.
4. A Final Clause.
5. A Relative Clause.

XXXIX*d*

Draw an imaginary plan to illustrate what you think the scene of the fighting described above (first paragraph) must have been like.

XL*a*

Give an English derivative from each of the following words:

Hostis—Credo—Relinquo—Video—Sequor—Impetus—Gravis—Manus—Traho—Tempus.

(Where verbs occur, derivatives may be from their compounds.)

XL*b*

When this exercise has been translated viva voce, write it out in as good English as you can. Keep the translation as literal as is consistent with *natural* English idiom.

XLI*a*

From this piece, *parse* (giving the Principal Parts of Verbs and the Genitive Singular and Gender of Nouns, and the meaning) the following words:

1. Accepisset.	2. Equites.	3. Eādem.
4. Avertatis.	5. Accidit.	6. Referte.
7. Primae.	8. Interfectis.	

XLI*b*

When this piece has been read aloud to you *twice in Latin*, write out in your own words or explain viva voce the gist of it *in English.*

XLII

(Before doing this piece, read the paragraphs on 'Connection in Latin Prose', which will be found on p. xvi.)

Translate into Latin:

On the Ides of March, Caesar was at first unwilling to leave his house, but in the end he went to the Senate House. As he went in, a man gave him a note, but he did not read it. When he had gone in, the conspirators, who had approached him by a trick, stood round him. Finally, wounded by many a hand, he fell before Pompey's statue.

XLIII

Re-write the following sentences with only *one main verb.*

1. Augustus gravem valetudinem passus est et infirmitatem magna cura tuebatur.
2. Urbem latericiam invenit et marmoream reliquit.
3. Lecticā clausā vehebatur; nam salutationes evitare voluit.
4. Febre corripi noluit; rarissime igitur se lavabat.
5. Provincias legibus justis administravit, imperium Romanum longa pace confirmavit.

XLIV

Make the following series of statements into a connected piece of Latin Prose:

Quintilius Varus Germaniam administravit. Dicebat oportere barbaros jure mulceri. Arminius Cheruscorum juvenis erat. Consilium rebellionis iniit. Insidias paravit. Legiones Romanae in hiberna reducebantur. Arminius eos circumvenit. Illi impedimenta reliquerunt. Per paludes aegre contenderunt. Tandem omnes perierunt.

XLV

When this piece has been read to you *twice in Latin*, write out (in your own words) the gist of it in English.

XLVI

This piece is a character-sketch of the Emperor Vespasian. Find out the answers to the following questions:

1. His elder son succeeded him as Emperor. What was this son's name?
2. What great city did this son sack in A.D. 70?
3. What great amphitheatre was built under Vespasian and his two sons?
4. What volcano erupted in A.D. 79?
5. Name one town buried by the eruption.
6. What was the name of Vespasian's younger son, Emperor after his brother?

XLVII

From the vocabulary of this piece, and using the subject-matter if desired, compose sentences in Latin to illustrate:

1. A Relative Clause.
2. An Ablative Absolute.
3. An Indirect Question.
4. A Final Clause.
5. An Indirect Command.

XLVIII

After this piece has been translated, give a short summary (in English) of the achievements of Agricola in Britain.

XLIX

Answer the following questions in Latin. In each answer, include a *main verb* and introduce *at least one* of the constructions dealt with in this book:

1. Qualia ad dominum referre Plinius solebat?
2. Quando coibant Christiani et quid facturi?
3. Quid accusatos jussit Plinius facere?
4. Quos Romam remittere constituit?
5. Qua de re Plinius magnopere haesitavit?

L

Re-write the following sentences with a different construction for the parts in italics:

1. Tum *hominem* in Foro *nudari jussit.*
2. *Dum* nomen civitatis *implorat,* crux homini comparatur.
3. *Sacerdotes vocantur,* rogantur quomodo simulacrum ablatum sit.

LI

Give an English derivative from each of the following words:

Urbs—Signo—Scio—Mille—Judicium—Plausus—Licet—Officium—Gero—Rego.

(Where verbs occur, derivatives may be from their compounds.)

LII

When this piece has been translated, write down *in Latin* and *in the third person* six events in the author's day.

LIII

On the basis of this piece, describe in your own words *in Latin* a performance at the Games (*Ludi*). Do this in simple sentences, but try to bring in one or two subordinate clauses, and make your Latin as connected as possible.

LIV

Translate the following passage into Latin:

Papirius, asked by his mother what the Senators had conferred about, said he was not allowed to tell. Asked again he told a lie and said that they had consulted whether a man ought to have two wives or a woman two husbands. Collecting the other married women, the mother went to the Senate House. Papirius therefore explained the whole matter and was praised by the Senators.

LV

Give an English derivative from each of the following words:

Peto — Amoenitas — Oculus — Capio — Pes — Copia — Invenio — Quantus—Quaero—Accido.

LVI

Re-write the following sentences so that they contain only *one main verb*:

1. Domus deserta est neque quisquam eam emere volebat.
2. In prima parte domus sedet; lumen poscit.
3. Servos dimittit; in pugillaribus aliquid scribit.
4. Audit vinculorum strepitum; non oculos tollit.

Why does Pliny prefer to use so many short sentences, each with its finite verb?

LVII

Vergil wrote this. Find out:

1. When he was born.
2. From what part of Italy he came.
3. What great work (in 12 books) he wrote.

LVIII

This refers to Quintus Fabius Maximus. Find out:

1. Against what enemy of Rome he fought.
2. Of what nationality that enemy was.
3. Who finally defeated that enemy in 202 B.C.
4. At what battle.

LIX

Cicero wrote this. Find out:

1. In what year he was consul.
2. Whose conspiracy he put down in that year.
3. The name of any one speech he wrote.
4. The year in which he died.
5. What famous man was responsible for his death.

LXXV

This was written by the Emperor Hadrian.

1. What great monument did he leave in Britain?
2. What was the date of his reign?

SUPPLEMENTARY EXERCISES FOR REVISION

The following exercises may be used for purposes of revision. They will, in each instance, deal with constructions up to and including the point named. So that they may be used later than the exercises which accompany each piece of Latin, they will include words from the Special Vocabularies up to a point somewhat ahead of the exercises with which they correspond in construction. This point is also named.

D. (*Relative Clauses.* Vocab. to Ex. X)

1. Does the name please you which your father gave you?
2. He alone began to complain when we were waiting-for food.
3. We then abandoned the trench we had prepared.
4. Those men are driving away the birds we are trying to catch.
5. A sudden storm arose and they could not endure it.
6. Here is a ditch: you will be safe in it.
7. Have you found the gate he will be coming to?
8. She was looking-for the son of a man she had seen in her own country.
9. This is a bold plan about which you have told me.
10. That is the river from which the soldiers will advance.

E. (*Ablative Absolute.* Vocab. to Ex. XVII)

1. He left his wife and children and came-back alone.
2. When the terms were learnt, the anger of all was-obvious.
3. A few were saved: the rest died in-misery (adj.).
4. As summer was beginning, many flowers were seen.
5. The way being-open, they found the safety they sought.
6. (He) who runs away can fight again.
7. The door was shut, so we stayed in the prison.
8. When children are silent, we expect danger.
9. He secretly imprisoned them and so averted accident.
10. We will start to-day with Caesar as our guide.

F. (*Indirect Statement.* Vocab. to Ex. XXIV)

1. He killed one old man and said he would kill another.
2. The stranger you see says he has never been to his native-land.
3. The king promised he would send away his friend and call in the ambassador.
4. They heard the signal, but refused to start.
5. As light was approaching, the woman said a new day was-at-hand.

6. The general knew the cavalry were eager, but he did not want to advance.
7. Do you say that you are collecting a lot of money?
8. This swamp, which is troubling the enemy, is a large one.
9. You all say the other lake is larger.
10. Does he understand that the tower is new?

G. (*Mixed Participles.* Vocab. to Ex. XXVI*b*)

1. Each, when summoned, said he was not worthy.
2. The soldier took a trumpet and pretended he was giving the signal.
3. We enjoyed our food and realised that we had been well nourished.
4. He released the stranger and sent him home.
5. (Though) filled with joy, my son nevertheless knew that sorrow was at hand.
6. When the people were complaining, the consul said he would help them.

H. (*Use of Cases.* Vocab. to Ex. XXIX)

1. Most men think bronze worth less than silver.
2. He said he would spare me for one hour.
3. The trick you have prepared is worthy of a better cause.
4. At Rome we ought to do what the Romans themselves do.
5. The stranger was saying he would reach Locri in two days.
6. Promise that you will come with us to-day.
7. At last, with great difficulty, he escaped-from slavery.
8. The river you see is twenty feet deep.

J. (*Final Clauses.* Vocab. to Ex. XXXIV*b*)

1. To enjoy that book, you ought to read it twice.
2. He entrusted the spoils to you, so that no one should touch them.
3. We are trying to keep-in-hiding, *to avoid* betraying ourselves.
4. Change your plans, *in-hopes-of* winning a great reward.
5. Being despised by all, he said he couldn't stay in the city.
6. Show this to the ambassador, *to make him* recognise you.
7. Having discovered the yokel, he said he would spare him.
8. They waited eight hours, in order to refresh themselves with sleep.

K. (*Indirect Commands.* Vocab. to Ex. XXXVIII)

1. I told the priest to collect everything except this.
2. He was telling his comrade not to avenge him.
3. The general is urging his men to take the mound by storm.

4. Britons often say that an opportunity is golden.
5. Meanwhile he ordered us to jump into that ditch unarmed.
6. I advise you to break-out to-day, to prevent the enemy blocking your way.
7. Tell the pirates to hurry to Miletus.
8. We kept awake all night to look-at the moon.

L. (*Indirect Questions.* Vocab. to Ex. XLIV)

1. He is asking whether most of you think that this corn is suitable.
2. I do not yet know whether my horse has been lost or not.
3. My wife was asking how the Britons lived only on meat and milk.
4. He doubted whether we had ever approved of the statue.
5. The conspirators complained that they had always been made to obey harsh laws.
6. Do you know if these men have one house each?
7. When their baggage had been lost, most of them never went outside the camp.
8. He asked whether they had entered the building and removed the bones.

The remaining exercises cover all the constructions included in this book.

M. (Vocab. to Ex. L)

1. They were sowing trees near the house, so that their children might avoid the sun.
2. He has embarked on that ship which was for a long time waiting at Gades.
3. They are asking whether, with the food failing, they can avoid disease.
4. You think that your services bring you gratitude from your friends.
5. I advise you to hide the dagger you have bought.
6. He laid the birds out on the ground; then prepared them for a feast.
7. I asked whether the fire was burning sufficiently.
8. We have been trying to discover whether he is wounded or dead.
9. The ghost urged him to commit this theft.
10. He realises that, when captured, he will suffer much pain.
11. The Emperor almost persuaded them to beg for pardon.
12. With great foresight he again sought the consulship.

N. (Vocab. to Ex. LVI)

1. Having crossed the threshold, the fat man told us that he was in need of food.
2. My neighbour asked whether I was starting out to-day or to-morrow.
3. Tell him to look at the snow on the hills.
4. When his business was completed, he walked to the city.
5. He opened the window, went out and walked for an hour.
6. Do you wonder whether she wants to marry you or not?
7. Sometimes fear compels him to run with great zeal.
8. To-morrow I shall have the reward I hoped I would have.
9. Not even learned men always want to study books.
10. The crowd seized his chariot so that he should not escape.
11. He advised his son to seek the companionship of good men.
12. He was showing me with his finger where fishes could be bought.

O. (Vocab. to end)

1. These tribes buy skins to clothe their limbs.
2. We delayed for an hour, then set out for London.
3. Either loyalty or love will compel us to help our friends.
4. My son was born in the city and is afraid of the sea.
5. I remember you told me not to set so much store by riches.
6. You cannot wonder why flowers flourish in this gentle land.
7. He warned me not to entrust my raft to the cruel sea.
8. My father bought a shield and painted an enormous dragon on it.

VOCABULARY I

VOCABULARY OF WORDS ASSUMED TO BE PREVIOUSLY KNOWN

a, ab (prep.), *by, from*
abeo, -ire, -ii, -itum, *go away, depart*
absum, -esse, -fui, *be absent, be away*
ac (conj.), *and*
accipio, -ere, -cepi, -ceptum, *receive, accept, take*
ad (prep.), *to, towards*
adsum, -esse, -fui, *be present, be at hand*
agricola, -ae (masc.), *farmer*
alius (adj.), *another*; **alii...alii**, *some...others*
altus (adj.), *high, tall, deep*
amo, -are, -avi, -atum, *love, be fond of, like*
amor, -is (masc.), *love, affection, liking*
annus, -i (masc.), *year*
ante (adv. and prep.), *before, in front (of)*
aqua, -ae (fem.), *water*
arma, -orum (neut.), *arms, weapons*
atque (conj.), *and*
audio, -ire, -ivi, -itum, *hear, listen to*
aurum, -i (neut.), *gold*

barbarus, -i (masc.), *barbarian*; as adj., *foreign, barbarian*
bellum, -i (neut.), *war*
bene (adv.), *well*
bonus (adj.), *good*
brevis (adj.), *short, brief*

caelum, -i (neut.), *sky, heaven, climate*
campus, -i (masc.), *plain*
carmen, -inis (neut.), *song, poem, ode, incantation*
castra, -orum (neut.), *camp*
causa, -ae (fem.), *cause, reason, case*
celeriter (adv.), *swiftly, quickly*
centum (num.), *a hundred*
circa (adv. and prep.), *about, around*
circum (adv. and prep.), *around, round*
civis, -is (masc.), *citizen*
consul, -is (masc.), *consul* (a Roman magistrate)
contra (adv. and prep.), *against, in opposition to, on the other hand*
copia, -ae (fem.), *plenty, abundance, supply*; pl. *forces, troops*
cornu, -us (neut.), *horn, wing of an army*
corpus, -oris (neut.), *body*
cum (prep.), *with*
cum (conj.), *when, since, because*
curro, -ere, cucurri, cursum, *run*

de (prep.), *from, down from, concerning, about*
dea, -ae (fem.), *goddess*
decem (num.), *ten*
descendo, -ere, -di, -sum, *go down, descend*
desum, -esse, -fui, *be missing, be lacking, fail*
deus, -i (masc.), *god*
dico, -ere, dixi, -ctum, *say, tell, talk*
dies, -ei (masc.), *day*
difficilis (adj.), *hard, difficult*
divido, -ere, -visi, -visum, *divide, separate*
do, dare, dedi, datum, *give, present*
dominus, -i (masc.), *lord, master*
donum, -i (neut.), *gift, present*
duco, -ere, duxi, ductum, *lead*
duo (num.), *two*
duodecim (num.), *twelve*
dux, -cis (masc.), *general, leader, guide*

e, ex (prep.), *out of, from*
ego (pron.), *I*
enim (conj.), *for*
eo, ire, ivi or ii, itum, *go*
equus, -i (masc.), *horse*
et (conj.), *and*
exercitus, -us (masc.), *army*
extra (adv. and prep.), *outside*

facilis (adj.), *easy*
facio, -ere, feci, factum, *do, perform, make*
femina, -ae (fem.), *woman, wife*
ferrum, -i (neut.), *iron, sword*
filia, -ae (fem.), *daughter*

finis, -is (masc.), *end*, *finish*; pl. *boundaries*, *territory*
fio, fieri, factus, *become*, *be made*
flos, -ris (masc.), *flower*
fortis (adj.), *brave*, *strong*
frater, -ris (masc.), *brother*

gladius, -i (masc.), *sword*
gravis (adj.), *heavy*, *serious*, *important*

habeo, -ēre, -ui, -itum, *have*, *possess*
hasta, -ae (fem.), *spear*
hic, haec, hoc (pron.), *this*, *he*, *she*, *it*
hiems, -is (fem.), *winter*
homo, -inis (masc.), *man*, *mankind*
hostis, -is (masc.), *enemy* (usually in pl.)

igitur (conj.), *therefore*
ille, illa, illud (pron.), *that*, *he*, *she*, *it*
impero, -are, -avi, -atum, *order*, *command*, *rule*
impetus, -us (masc.), *charge*, *attack*, *force*
in (prep.), with Acc., *into*, *against*; with Abl., *in*, *on*
ineo, -ire, -ii, -itum, *enter*, *go in*
infra (adv. and prep.), *below*, *under*, *underneath*
inquam, -quit (verb), *I say*, *he says*
inter (prep.), *between*, *among*
intra (adv. and prep.), *inside*
intro, -are, -avi, -atum, *enter*, *go in*
is, ea, id (pron.), *that*, *he*, *she*, *it*
iste, -a, -ud (pron.), *that over there*, *that of yours*

jam (adv.), *now*, *already*
jubeo, -ēre, jussi, jussum, *order*, *command*, *tell*
juvenis, -is (masc.), *young man*, *youth*; as adj., *young*

lăbor, -oris (masc.), *work*, *toil*, *labour*
laudo, -are, -avi, -atum, *praise*, *commend*
laus, -dis (fem.), *praise*, *reputation*
lavo, -are, lavi, lautum or lotum, *wash*
legio, -onis (fem.), *legion* (generally 6000 men)
locus, -i (masc.), *place*
longus (adj.), *long*, *lengthy*
ludo, -ere, lusi, lusum, *play*, *sport*

magis (adv.), *more*, *to a greater extent*
magnus (adj.), *large*, *great*
major (adj.), *larger*, *greater*
male (adv.), *badly*, *evilly*, *ill*
malo, malle, malui, *prefer*
malus (adj.), *bad*, *evil*
mare, -is (neut.), *sea*
mater, -ris (fem.), *mother*
maximus (adj.), *largest*, *greatest*
medius (adj.), *middle*, *centre*
memoria, -ae (fem.), *memory*, *remembrance*
meus (possess. pron.), *my*, *mine*
miles, -itis (masc.), *soldier*
minime (adv.), *least*, *in the smallest degree*
minor (adj.), *smaller*, *lesser*, *less*
moenia, -ium (neut.), *walls*, *city-walls*
moneo, -ēre, -ui, -itum, *warn*, *advise*
mora, -ae (fem.), *delay*
moveo, -ēre, movi, motum, *move* (trans.)
mox (adv.), *presently*, *in due course*
multus (adj.), *much*, *many*

nam, **namque** (conj.), *for*
nauta, -ae (masc.), *sailor*
navis, -is (fem.), *ship*, *boat*
ne (conj.), *not*, *in order that not*, *for fear that*
nec, **neque** (conj.), *neither*, *nor*, *and not*
nego, -are, -avi, -atum, *deny*, *say that not*
nihil (neut.), *nothing*
nisi (conj.), *unless*, *if not*, *except*
nobilis (adj.), *noble*, *of good birth*
nolo, nolle, nolui, *be unwilling*, *refuse*
non (adv.), *not*
nos (pron.), *we*
noster (adj.), *our*
nox, -ctis (fem.), *night*
nullus (adj.), *no*, *none*
nuntio, -are, -avi, -atum, *announce*, *tell*, *proclaim*
nuntius, -i (masc.), *messenger*, *message*

ob (prep.), *on account of*, *in the way of*, *because of*
obeo, -ire, -ii, -itum, *go in the way of*, *meet*, *undergo*
occīdo, -ere, -cidi, -cisum, *slay*, *kill*, *put to death*
omnis (adj.), *all*

oppidum, -i (neut.), *town*
optimus (adj.), *best*
opus, -eris (neut.), *work, task*
oratio, -ionis (fem.), *speech, oratory*
ordo, -inis (masc.), *order, arrangement*
os, oris (neut.), *face, mouth, entrance*

pars, -tis (fem.), *part*
parvus (adj.), *small, little*
pater, -ris (masc.), *father*
pax, -cis (fem.), *peace*
per (prep.), *through, by means of, on account of*
pessimus (adj.), *worst*
plurimus (adj.), *most, very many*
plus (adv.), *more*
possum, posse, potui, *be able, can*
post (adv. and prep.), *after, afterwards, behind*
postquam (conj.), *after*
postremus (adj.), *hindmost, last*
primus (adj.), *first, foremost*
pro (prep.), *in front of, instead of, on behalf of*
prohibeo, -ēre, -ui, -itum, *prevent, stop*
prope (adv. and prep.), *near*
proximus (adj.), *nearest, latest, last*
puella, -ae (fem.), *girl, maiden*
puer, -i (masc.), *boy, lad*
pugna, -ae (fem.), *fight, battle*
pugno, -are, -avi, -atum, *fight, do battle*
punio, -ire, -ivi, -itum, *punish*
puto, -are, -avi, -atum, *think, consider, imagine*

quam (adv.), *how*; *as*; *than*
quantus (adj.), *how much, how large, how great*; *as much, as large, as great*
quattuor (num.), *four*
qui, quae, quod (pron.), *who, which*
quidam (pron.), *a certain, a*
quinquaginta (num.), *fifty*
quintus (adj.), *fifth*
quis, quid (interrog. pron.), *who, what*
quod (conj.), *because*
quoque (adv.), *also*
quum (conj.), see **cum** (conj.)

recipio, -ere, -cepi, -ceptum, *receive, take back*
reddo, -ere, reddidi, -itum, *give back, return*
regnum, -i (neut.), *kingdom, reign, kingship*
res, rei (fem.), *thing, matter, affair*
respublica, reipublicae (fem.), *public affairs, politics, commonwealth, state*
rex, regis (masc.), *king, monarch*
rogo, -are, -avi, -atum, *ask, beg, request*

sacer (adj.), *sacred, holy*
scio, -ire, -ivi, -itum, *know, know how to* (with Infin.)
scribo, -ere, -psi, -ptum, *write, draw*
scutum, -i (neut.), *shield*
se (reflex. pron.), *himself, themselves*
sed (conj.), *but*
septem (num.), *seven*
septimus (adj.), *seventh*
servus (masc.), *slave, servant*
sex (num.), *six*
sextus (adj.), *sixth*
si (conj.), *if*
sic (adv.), *thus, so*
silva, -ae (fem.), *wood, copse*
sine (prep.), *without*
socius, -i (masc.), *ally, partner, companion*
spero, -are, -avi, -atum, *hope, hope for, expect*
sto, -are, steti, statum, *stand*
sub (prep.), with Acc., *up to and under*; with Abl., *under, below*
sum, esse, fui, *be, exist*
summus (adj.), *top, highest, topmost*
super (prep. and adv.), *above, on top, on top of*
superior (adj.), *higher, superior, former*
suus (possess. pron.), *his own, their own*; pl. **sui**, *his men*

tam (adv.), *so*
tamen (conj.), *however*
tandem (adv.), *at length, at last*
telum, -i (neut.), *javelin, weapon*
templum, -i (neut.), *temple, sanctuary, shrine*
tempus, -oris (neut.), *time, occasion*; pl. (often) *forehead, temples*
teneo, -ēre, -ui, tentum, *hold, grasp, grip*
ter (num. adv.), *three times, thrice*
terra, -ae (fem.), *earth, land*

tertius (adj.), *third*
timeo, -ēre, -ui, *be afraid (of), fear*
timor, -is (masc.), *fear*
totus (adj.), *whole, all*
trans (prep.), *across, over*
tres (num.), *three*
triginta (num.), *thirty*
tristis (adj.), *sad, sorrowful, gloomy*
tu (pron.), *thou, you* (sing.)
tum (adv.), *then, subsequently, at that time*
tuus (possess. pron.), *thine, your*

ubi (adv.), *where, when*
unda, -ae (fem.), *wave, water*
undecimus (adj.), *eleventh*
unus (num.), *one, only*
urbs, -is (fem.), *city*
usus, -us (masc.), *use, practice, familiarity*
ut (conj.), *in order that, so that*; *as, when*
utilis (adj.), *useful*
utor, -i, usus, *make use of, use, employ*

ventus, -i (masc.), *wind*
verbum, -i (neut.), *word*
vester (possess. pron.), *your* (pl.)
vestis, -is (fem.), *clothes, clothing, dress*
via, -ae (fem.), *road, way, route*
video, -ēre, vidi, visum, *see, perceive*
viginti (num.), *twenty*
vinculum, -i (neut.), *link, bond, cable*
vinum, -i (neut.), *wine*
vir, -i (masc.), *man, husband*
virgo, -inis (fem.), *maiden, girl*
vis, vis (fem.), *force, power, violence*; pl. vires, *strength*
vita, -ae (fem.), *life*
vivo, -ere, vixi, victum, *live*
vix (adv.), *scarcely, barely*
voco, -are, -avi, -atum, *call, summon*
volo, velle, volui, *wish, want, be willing*
vos (pron.), *you* (pl.)

VOCABULARY II

abdo, -ere, -didi, -ditum, *hide, conceal*

abduco, -ere, -xi, -ctum, *lead off, lead aside*

abjicio, -ere, -jeci, -jectum, *throw away, reject*

abripio, -ere, -ripui, -reptum, *snatch, seize, tear away*

abscindo, -ere, -scidi, -scissum, *tear away, cut off*

absolvo, -ere, -solvi, -solutum, *release, loose, excuse*

abstinentia, -ae (fem.), *restraint, holding off, abstinence*

abstineo, -ēre, -ui, -tentum, *hold off, abstain*

abstraho, -ere, -traxi, -ctum, *draw off, draw away*

abundo, XXXIX *b*

accido, LV

accubo, -are, -ui, -itum, *lie at the side of, lie (near the table) for dinner*

accusator, -is (masc.), *accuser, prosecutor*

acer, XVIII

acerbus, L *b*

acies, VII

acriter (adv.), *keenly, fiercely, vigorously*

adduco, -ere, -xi, -ctum, *lead up, lead towards*

adfero, -ferre, -tuli, -latum (aff-), *bring up, bring towards*

adficio, -ere, -feci, -fectum (aff-), *affect, treat*

adfigo, -ere, -fixi, -fixum (aff-), *fasten to, attach*

adfirmo, -are, -avi, -atum (aff-), *affirm, maintain, declare*

adfligo, -ere, -flixi, -flictum (aff-), *afflict, punish*

adgredior, -i, -gressus (agg-), *approach, attack*

adhuc (adv.), *so far, hitherto, to this point, still*

adipiscor, XXXIV *b*

aditus, -us (masc.), *approach, entrance*

adjuvo, -are, -juvi, -jutum, *help, aid, assist*

adloquor, -i, -locutus (all-), *talk to, address, speak to*

admiratio, -ionis (fem.), *admiration, surprise, wonder*

admitto, -ere, -misi, -missum, *let in, admit, commit (a crime)*

admoveo, -ēre, -movi, -motum, *move up, bring up*

adnuo, -ere, -nui, -nutum (ann-), *nod to, consent, say yes*

adparatus (adj.) (app-), *ready, prepared, elaborate*

adpareo, -ēre, -ui, -itum, *appear*

adpello, -ere, -puli, -pulsum (app-), *drive towards, bring to berth (a ship)*

adpono, -ere, -posui, -itum (app-), *set by, place near*

adprehendo, -ere, -di, -sum (app-), *catch, seize, understand*

adprobo, -are, -avi, -atum (app-), *approve*

adripio, -ere, -ui, -reptum (arr-), *seize to one's self*

adscendo, -ere, -di, -sum (asc-), *mount, ascend, go up*

adsevero, -are, -avi, -atum (ass-), *maintain, declare*

adsto, -are, -stiti, -stitum (ast-), *stand near, be at hand*

adsuesco, -ere, -evi, -etum (ass-), *accustom*

adsuetus (adj.) (ass-), *accustomed, usual*

adsumo, -ere, -mpsi, -mptum (ass-), *take up, assume*

adtineo, -ēre, -ui, -tentum (att-), *reach, attain*

adtingo, -ere, -tigi, -tactum (att-), *touch, reach*

adulatio, -ionis (fem.), *flattery*

adulescens, -tis (masc.), *youth, young man*

adulescentia, -ae (fem.), *youth, adolescence, early manhood*

adulterium, -i (neut.), *adultery*

advenio, -ire, -veni, -ventum, *come up, come to, arrive*

adventus, -us (masc.), *arrival, approach*

adversarii, -orum (masc.), *opponents, rivals*

adversus (adv.), *against, towards*

aedificium, XL *b*

aeger, XLVII

aegre (adv.), *scarcely, barely, hardly*

aequor, LX
aequus, XLIII
aes, XXVII
aestas, XI
aestimo, XXXVIII
aetas, XXXVIII
aeternus (adj.), *everlasting, eternal*
aevum, LVI
agger, XXXV
agmen, VII
agnosco, XXXIV *b*
ago, XLVIII
agrestis, XXXI
albeo, -ēre, *be white, be fair (in colour)*
albus (adj.), *white*
aliquando, LII
aliquis, XLII
alo, XIII *b*
alter, XV
altitudo, -inis (fem.), *height, depth*
ambo (adj.), *both*
ambulo, LII
amicitia, -ae (fem.), *friendship, affection*
amicus, XVII
amitto, XLIV
amoenitas, -atis (fem.), *pleasantness, amenity*
amoenus, LXV
amputo, -are, -avi, -atum, *prune, cut off*
an, *or* (second half of double question)
ancilla, -ae (fem.), *maidservant, female slave*
ancora, -ae (fem.), *anchor*
anguis, -is (comm.), *snake, serpent*
angulus, -i (masc.), *corner, angle*
angustiae, XIV *a*
animula, -ae (fem., dimin. of anima), *soul, spirit*
animus, XII
anser, -is (masc.), *goose*
antea (adv.), *before, previously*
antecedo, -ere, -cessi, -cessum, *go before, precede*
Antiensis (adj.), *of the town of Antium*
antiquus, L *b*
aper, -ri (masc.), *boar*
aperio, LII
appello, -are, XIX
appropinquo, VII
apud, XLI *b*
aquilifer, *standard-bearer*
aquosus (adj.), *watery, rainy*
arbitror, XXXIX *a*
arbor, IV
arcesso, XXIV
ardeo, L *a*
area, -ae (fem.), *courtyard, threshing-floor*
argentum, XXVII
argumentum, -i (neut.), *proof*
armo, -are, -avi, -atum, *arm, fit out*
arrogantia, -ae (fem.), *pride, overbearing, arrogance*
arx, -cis (fem.), *citadel, stronghold*
asper (adj.), *rough, harsh*
atrocitas, -atis (fem.), *fierceness, harshness, atrocity*
atrox (adj.), *harsh, fierce*
attonitus, XXXIII
auctor, XLIX *b*
auctoritas, XXVI *a*
audacia, -ae (fem.), *courage, daring, recklessness*
audax, I
audeo, XXXIX *c*
aufero, -ferre, abstuli, ablatum, *carry off, carry away*
augurium, -i (neut.), *augury, omen*
aureus, XXXV
auris, XL *b*
aut, XIX
auxilium, IX *b*
averto, -ere, -verti, -versum, *turn aside, avert*
avis, V

baculum, -i (neut.), *stick, walking-stick*
balineae, -arum (fem.), *public baths*
balineum, -i (neut.), *bath, public bath*
barba, LVI
bellua, -ae (fem.), *monster*
bestia, -ae (fem.), *beast*
blandulus (dimin. adj. of **blandus**), *gentle, kindly*
Britanni, -orum (masc.), *Britons*
Britannia, -ae (fem.), *Britain*

cadaver, -is (neut.), *corpse, body*
cado, -ere, cecidi, casum, *fall*
caedes, XXX
caedo, XXXIV *a*
caeruleus (adj.), *blue* (colour of sea or sky)

Caledonia, -ae (fem.), *Scotland*
calor, -is (masc.), *heat, warmth*
candelabrum, -i (neut.), *lamp-stand, candlestick*
Cantium, -i (neut.), *Kent*
capillus, -i (masc.), *hair* (usually in pl.)
capio, I
Capitolium, -i (neut.), *The Capitol*
captivus, -i (masc.), *prisoner, captive*
caput, XV
carcer, XVII
careo, XVI
caro, XXXIX *a*
carus (adj.), *dear*
castellum, -i (neut.), *fort, fortress*
casus, XVII
catena, LVI
Catinenses, -ium (masc.), *people of Catina*
caveo, XLII
caverna, -ae (fem.), *cave, cavern*
cedo, LXIII
celo, XLVII
cena, -ae (fem.), *dinner, feast, banquet*
ceno, -are, -avi, -atum, *dine, sup*
censor, -oris (masc.), *censor* (a Roman magistrate)
centurio, -ionis (masc.), *centurion* (an officer in the Roman army)
cerae, -arum (fem.), *wax tablets, notebook*
certus (adj.), *sure, certain, definite*
ceteri, XIII *a*
cibus, IX *b*
circenses, -ium (masc.), *public games, circus*
circulus, -i (masc.), *ring, circle*
circumeo, -ire, -ivi, -itum, *go round, encircle*
circumfero, -ferre, -tuli, -latum, *take round, carry round*
circumscribo, -ere, -scripsi, -scriptum, *draw round*
circumsto, -are, -stiti, *surround, encircle*
circumveho, -ere, -vexi, -vectum, *carry round*; pass. *ride* (or *sail*) *round*
circumvenio, -ire, -veni, -ventum, *go round, encircle*
Cisalpinus (adj.), *on this side of the Alps*
cito, -are, -avi, -atum, *rouse, stir, set at a gallop*
civilis (adj.), *civil, of the state*
civitas, VI
clades, -is (fem.), *disaster, defeat*
clam, XIII *b*
clamito, -are, -avi, -atum, *keep shouting, exclaim often*
clamo, -are, -avi, -atum, *shout, exclaim, say*
clamor, IV
clango, -ere, *make a noise, rattle*
clare (adv.), *clearly, obviously, loudly*
clarus (adj.), *clear, obvious, loud*
claudo, XIV *b*
clipeus, LXI
coeo, -ire, -ivi, -itum, *come together, collect*
coepi, X
coerceo, XLVIII
cognosco, XVI
cogo, XL *b*
cohors, -tis (fem.), *cohort*
collega, -ae (masc.), *colleague, partner*
colligo, XXI
collis, XXXV
colloquor, -i, -locutus, *confer, talk together, parley*
colo, -ere, -ui, cultum, *cultivate, till, worship*
colonus, -i (masc.), *farmer, tenant*
comes, XXXV
comitas, -atis (fem.), *pleasantness, courtesy*
comitium, -i (neut.), *meeting*; pl. *assembly, elections*
comito, -are, -avi, -atum, *accompany, go with*
commendo, -are, -avi, -atum, *commend, praise, recommend*
comminus (adv.), *at close quarters, hand to hand*
committo, -ere, -misi, -missum, *entrust, commit*; **committere proelium**, *join battle*
commodum, -i (neut.), *advantage, benefit*
communis, XL *b*
comoedus, -i (masc.), *comic actor, writer of comedies*
comparo, -are, -avi, -atum, *prepare, make ready, produce*
compello, -ere, -puli, -pulsum, *compel, force*
complector, -i, -plexus, *embrace, include*

compleo, XXV
compono, -ere, -posui, -positum, *compose, make up*
comprehendo, -ere, -ndi, -nsum, *arrest, seize, understand*
concito, -are, -avi, -atum, *rouse, stir*
concurro, XXIII
concutio, -ere, -cussi, -cussum, *shake up*
condicio, XIV *a*
condo, -ere, -didi, -ditum, *found, establish, hide*
confero, -ferre, -tuli, collatum, *compare, contribute, produce*
conficio, -ere, -feci, -fectum, *finish, end, conclude*
confirmo, XL *a*
confiteor, XLIX *b*
conflicto, -are, -avi, -atum, *strike, fight, ruin*
confodio, -ere, -fodi, -fossum, *dig out, stab*
confugio, -ere, -fugi, -fugitum, *flee, take to flight*
congratulor, -ari, -atus, *congratulate*
conjicio, -ere, -jeci, -jectum, *throw together, hurl*
conjuratus, XLII
conor, VIII
conscendo, XLV
consensus, -us (masc.), *agreement, harmony*
conservo, XLI *a*
consilium, I
consisto, XL *a*
conspicor, -ari, -atus, *see, catch sight of*
constans (adj.), *faithful, constant, enduring*
constantia, -ae (fem.), *endurance, perseverance*
constituo, IX *a*
consulatus, XLVIII
consulo, XXVIII
consumo, -ere, -mpsi, -mptum, *consume, take up, use up*
consurgo, -ere, -surrexi, -surrectum, *arise, get up*
contemno, XXX
contendo, XXI
contentio, -ionis (fem.), *effort, struggle, endeavour*
contero, -ere, -trivi, -tritum, *wear away, rub away, wear out*
contexo, -ere, -ui, -xtum, *weave together, join*
contineo, -ēre, -ui, -tentum, *contain, hold together*
continuus, XXVII
contrarius, XXXIX *b*
convenio, -ire, -veni, -ventum, *come together, assemble*
convivium, XLVI
convoco, -are, -avi, -atum, *call together, summon*
coram, XIX
corona, XXIII
corripio, -ere, -ui, -reptum, *seize, snatch*
corrumpo, -ere, -rupi, -ruptum, *corrupt, bribe*
cras, LI
credo, XIV *b*
cremo, -are, -avi, -atum, *burn, cremate*
creo, IX *b*
crepitus, -us (masc.), *creaking, noise*
crinis, -is (fem.), *hair* (usually in pl.)
crudelis, XVII
crux, -cis (fem.), *cross*
cubiculum, -i (neut.), *bedroom*
cubo, -are, -ui, -itum, *lie down, sleep*
culpo, -are, -avi, -atum, *blame*
cumulo, -are, -avi, -atum, *heap up, pile up*
cunctor, LVIII
cupiditas, -atis (fem.), *desire, greed*
cupido, LV
cupidus, LXVII
cupio, LIII
cur, XV
cura, XXII
curia, XXXVI
curo, XLVI
currus, LIII
cursor, -oris (masc.), *runner*
cursus, XXIV
custodia, -ae (fem.), *guard, protection*

damno, -are, -avi, -atum, *condemn, convict*
debello, -are, -avi, -atum, *defeat in war, conquer*
debeo, XXIII
decedo, -ere, -cessi, -cessum, *depart, go away, die*
decemvir, -i (masc.), *decemvir, a member of a board of ten*

decemviralis (adj.), *decemviral*
decet, -ēre, -uit, *it is fitting, it is becoming*
decido, -ere, -cidi, *fall down, collapse*
decimus (adj.), *tenth*
decipio, -ere, -cepi, -ceptum, *deceive, cheat*
declaro, -are, -avi, -atum, *declare, maintain, say*
decor, -is (masc.), *beauty*
decorus (adj.), *beautiful, becoming*
decumbo, -ere, -cubui, *lie down*
dedecus, XLI *a*
dedico, -are, -avi, -atum, *dedicate*
dedo, -ere, dedidi, deditum, *surrender, give up*
deduco, -ere, -duxi, -ductum, *lead aside, lead away*
defectio, -ionis (fem.), *revolt, rebellion, failure*
defendo, -ere, -ndi, -nsum, *defend, protect, ward off*
defero, L *b*
deficio, XLV
dein, deinde (adv.), *then, thereafter*
dejicio, -ere, -jeci, -jectum, *throw away, throw down, overthrow*
delabor, -i, -lapsus, *fall away, slip down*
delectatio, -ionis (fem.), *pleasure, delight*
delecto, -are, -avi, -atum, *please, delight*
deleo, XXX
delibero, -are, -avi, -atum, *consider, think over, deliberate*
deminuo, -ere, -ui, -utum, *lessen, diminish*
demitto, -ere, -misi, -missum, *send away, let down*
demonstro, XXXVI
demum, XXVIII
denique, XXVII
dens, XLIII
densus, XLIV
depono, -ere, -posui, -positum, *put down, set aside*
deseco, -are, -ui, -ctum, *cut up, cut to pieces*
desero, -ere, -ui, -rtum, *desert, abandon, give up*
desilio, XXXVII
despero, XL *a*
deveho, -ere, -vexi, -vectum, *carry down, carry away*
devoro, -are, -avi, -atum, *devour, consume, eat up*
dexter (adj.), *right, right-handed*
dictator, -is (masc.), *dictator* (a Roman magistrate)
dictatura, -ae (fem.), *dictatorship*
dictito, -are, -avi, -atum, *keep saying, say frequently*
dicto, -are, -avi, -atum, *say often, dictate, declare*
diduco, -ere, -duxi, -ductum, *lead aside, lead apart, draw aside*
digitus, LVI
dignus, XXV
dilabor, -i, -lapsus, *slip away, slip off*
diligentia, XLI *a*
dimico, XLI *b*
dimitto, -ere, -misi, -missum, *send away, dismiss*
diripio, -ere, -ripui, -reptum, *snatch away, tear apart*
discedo, XXVIII
disciplina, XLVI
disco, XLVIII
discordia, -ae (fem.), *discord, disagreement*
discrimen, XXXIII
dispello, -ere, -puli, -pulsum, *send away, drive away, dispel*
dispono, -ere, -posui, -itum, *arrange, dispose*
distraho, -ere, -traxi, -tractum, *draw aside, distract*
diu (comp. **diutius**, *longer, for a longer time*), XLVII
dives, XXXIV *b*
dolor, XXI
dolus, XXVII
domesticus (adj.), *belonging to home, domestic*
domo, -are, -ui, -itum, *tame, soften, bring under control*
domus, XXII
dormio, -ire, -ivi, -itum, *sleep*
dubito, XLII
dulcis, L *a*
dum, XXXI

eburneus (adj.), *made of ivory*
ĕdo, XLVI
ēdo, XXXIV *a*
edoceo, -ēre, -ui, -ctum, *teach thoroughly, teach by heart*
educo, -ere, -duxi, -ductum, *lead out*

effero, -ferre, extuli, elatum, *carry out, carry away*
efficio, -ere, -feci, -fectum, *perform, carry out, bring about*
effigies, LVI
effodio, -ere, -fodi, -fossum, *dig out*
egeo, XXVII
egredior, -i, -gressus, *go out, leave*
ejicio, -ere, -jeci, -jectum, *throw out, cast forth, throw*
elabor, -i, -lapsus, *slip out*
elegantia, -ae (fem.), *neatness, elegance*
elephantus, -i (masc.), *elephant*
eligo, -ere, -legi, -lectum, *choose (out), select, elect*
eloquens (adj.), *eloquent, fluent*
eloquentia, -ae (fem.), *eloquence, fluency*
emineo, -ēre, -ui, *stand out, be remarkable*
emo, XXVI*b*
emollio, -ire, -ivi, -itum, *make soft, soothe, quieten*
en (interjection), *lo!, behold!*
enarro, -are, -avi, -atum, *tell fully, relate*
enuntio, LIV
eques, XXI
ergo, XLIX*a*
erro, -are, -avi, -atum, *wander, be mistaken, err*
error, -is (masc.), *wandering, mistake*
eruditus, LII
erumpo, XXXVI
etiam (adv.), *also, even, still*
evenio, -ire, -veni, -ventum, *come out, result, happen*
evigilo, -are, -avi, -atum, *be watchful, be awake*
evito, -are, -avi, -atum, *avoid*
exactio, -ionis (fem.), *exaction, levying*
exanimus, XLII
excipio, -ere, -cepi, -ceptum, *take out, receive*
excito, XIII*b*
exclamo, -are, -avi, -atum, *exclaim, say, remark*
excludo, -ere, -si, -sum, *shut out, shut off, exclude*
exemplum, -i (neut.), *example*
exeo, -ire, -ii, -itum, *go out*
exerceo, XLIII
exitium, XXXIV*b*
expeditio, -ionis (fem.), *expedition*
expello, -ere, -puli, -pulsum, *drive out, expel*
explico, -are, -avi, -atum, *unfold, explain*
exploro, -are, -avi, -atum, *explore, reconnoitre*
expono, -ere, -posui, -itum, *put out, expose, explain, disembark* (act.)
expugno, XXXV
exseco, -are, -ui, -ctum, *cut up, cut out*
exsecror, -ari, -atus, *curse, call down a curse*
exspecto, VII
exspiro, -are, -avi, -atum, *faint, die, breathe out*
exstinguo, -ere, -xi, -ctum, *put out, extinguish*
exstruo, XLIII
extendo, -ere, -di, -sum, *stretch out, extend*
exterreo, -ēre, -ui, -itum, *terrify, frighten*
extollo, -ere, *lift up, lift out, praise*
extorqueo, -ēre, -si, -tum, *twist out, snatch*
extraho, -ere, -traxi, -tractum, *draw out, extract*
extremus, LIII

facies, XXXII
facultas, XXXII
fallo, -ere, fefelli, falsum, *deceive, cheat, mislead*
familia, -ae (fem.), *household, family*
fanum, -i (neut.), *shrine, sanctuary, temple*
fauces, -ium (fem.), *jaws, pass*
faveo, -ēre, favi, fautum, *favour*
favor, -is (masc.), *favour, kindness*
febris, -is (fem.), *fever, illness, temperature*
feliciter, XXIII
femineus (adj.), *feminine, belonging to a woman*
fenestra, LII
fere, ferme, XLIV
ferio, -ire, *strike, hit*
fero (ferunt, *men say*), IV
ferocitas, -atis (fem.), *fierceness, boldness*
fessus (adj.), *tired, weary*
fides, LXII
filius, II

fingo, XXVI*a*
firmo, -are, -avi, -atum, *strengthen*
flagro, -are, -avi, -atum, *burn, blaze*
flamma, -ae (fem.), *flame*
flecto, XXIX
fleo, X
floreo, LXXI
flumen, VIII
fluo, -ere, -xi, -xum, *flow*; *run* (of liquids)
fluvius, XLV
fodio, -ere, fodi, fossum, *dig*
foedus, XXXIX*b*
fores, -um (fem.), *door, double door*
forma, -ae (fem.), *beauty, form, shape*
formo, -are, -avi, -atum, *form, shape, make*
forte, XXVIII
forum, L*a*
fossa, IX*a*
foveo, -ēre, fovi, fotum *or* fautum, *cherish, look after*
fragilis (adj.), *breakable, fragile*
fragor, -oris (masc.), *noise, crash*
fragro, -are, -avi, -atum, *smell*
frango, -ere, fregi, fractum, *break, smash*
fraus, -dis (fem.), *deception, trick, fraud*
fremitus, -us (masc.), *raging, roaring, noise*
frequento, -are, -avi, -atum, *frequent, be about*
fretus (adj.), *relying on, dependent on*
frons, -tis (fem.), *front, forehead*
fructus, LI
frumentum, XXXIX*a*
fruor, XXVI*a*
fuga, XIX
fugio, XXII
fugo, -are, -avi, -atum, *rout, put to flight*
fundo, XLI*b*
furor, L*a*
furtum, XLIX*a*

Galli, -orum (masc.), *Gauls*
Gallia, -ae (fem.), *Gaul*
gaudium, -i (neut.), *joy, pleasure, gladness*
gens, XLVIII
genus, XXXI
gero, XVII
gigno, -ere, genui, -itum, *beget, be father of, produce*
gladiatorius (adj.), *gladiatorial*
gradus, LVI
Graecia, -ae (fem.), *Greece*
Graecus (adj.), *Greek*
gramen, LXXII
gratia, XXIII
gratulatio, -ionis (fem.), *congratulation, praise*
gratus (adj.), *pleasing, grateful, influential*
gravitas, -atis (fem.), *heaviness, seriousness, dignity*
gremium, -i (neut.), *lap, bosom*
gurges, -itis (masc.), *whirlpool, eddy*

haereo, LI
haesitatio, -ionis (fem.), *hesitation, doubt*
haesito, -are, -avi, -atum, *hesitate, be in doubt*
haud (adv.), *not*
haurio, -ire, hausi, haustum, *drain, drink, exhaust*
herba, -ae (fem.), *grass, greensward, herb*
herbidus (adj.), *grassy, herbaceous*
heri, LV
hiberna, XLIV
Hibernia, -ae (fem.), *Ireland*
hic (adv.), *here, at this point*
Hispania, -ae (fem.), *Spain*
hodie, XV
hora, XVIII
horreo, -ēre, -ui, *be frightened, bristle*
horribilis (adj.), *terrible, frightening*
hortor, XXX
hortus, LV
hospes, XXII
hospitalis (adj.), *of a stranger, of a guest, hospitable*
hospitium, -i (neut.), *hospitality, entertainment*
huc (adv.), *hither, up to this point*
humanus (adj.), *human*
humerus, see **umerus**

ibi, XIII*a*
ictus (participle), see **ferio**
ictus, -us (masc.), *blow, stroke*
idem, V
idoneus, XLIV
Idus, -uum (fem.), *the Ides* (15th of March, May, July, October; 13th of other months)

ignavia, -ae (fem.), *cowardice, laziness*
ignis, VIII
ignominia, -ae (fem.), *disgrace, ignominy*
ignoro, -are, -avi, -atum, *be unaware, not know*
ignosco, -ere, -novi, -notum, *pardon, excuse, forgive*
ignotus, XLIX *a*
imago, XLIX *a*
imber, XXXIX *b*
imitor, -ari, -atus, *imitate, copy*
immensus (adj.), *unmeasurable, huge, vast*
immergo, -ere, -si, -sum, *dip, plunge in, sink*
immitto, -ere, -misi, -missum, *send in*
immodicus (adj.), *immoderate, unreasonable*
immortalis (adj.), *immortal, deathless*
immotus (adj.), *unmoved*
impedimentum, XLIV
impello, -ere, -puli, -pulsum, *drive in, urge*
imperator, XL *a*
imperatorius (adj.), *of a general*
imperium, XL *b*
impetro, X
impleo, -ēre, -evi, -etum, *fill*
implico, -are, -ui, -itum, *involve, fold in*
imploro, -are, -avi, -atum, *implore, beg, beseech*
impono, -ere, -posui, -itum, *put in, put on, impose*
importo, -are, -avi, -atum, *bring in, import*
improvisus (adj.), *unforeseen, unexpected*
impune (adv.), *unpunished, without punishment*
inanis, LI
incendium, XXXVI
incendo, X
incertus (adj.), *uncertain, unsure*
incipio, II
incola, -ae (masc.), *inhabitant*
incolo, XXXIX *a*
incolumis, VIII
incultus (adj.), *uncultivated, not cared for*
incutio, -ere, -cussi, -cussum, *strike against, inspire, excite*
index, -icis (comm.), *informer*
indico, XLII
indignus (adj.), *unworthy, undeserved, undeserving*
induo, -ere, -ui, -utum, *put on*
industria, -ae (fem.), *hard work, industry*; **de industria**, *on purpose*
inermis, XXXVI
inertia, -ae (fem.), *laziness, inactivity, slackness*
infans, -tis (comm.), *infant, baby*
infelix, XXXIX *d*
infirmitas, -atis (fem.), *weakness, illness*
infirmus (adj.), *weak, ill*
ingenium, XXVIII
ingens, XIX
ingratus (adj.), *unpleasing, ungrateful*
ingredior, -i, -gressus, *enter, go in*
inhonestus (adj.), *dishonourable, disgraceful*
inimicus (adj.), *hostile*; as noun, *enemy*
injicio, -ere, -jeci, -jectum, *throw in, put in, inject*
injuria, VI
innocens (adj.), *innocent, harmless*
innuo, -ere, -ui, -utum, *nod to, beckon*
inruo, -ere, -ui (irr-), *rush in, attack*
inscius (adj.), *unknowing, unaware, ignorant*
insequor, -i, -secutus, *pursue, persecute, threaten*
insidiae, XIV *a*
insisto, -ere, -stiti, -stitum, *threaten, pursue, stand in*
insolenter (adv.), *unusually, proudly, arrogantly*
inspicio, -ere, -spexi, -ctum, *look into, look on, watch*
instituo, -ere, -ui, -utum, *set up, establish, begin*
instruo, XXI
insula, XXXVIII
insulto, -are, -avi, -atum, *jump on, insult*
insurgo, -ere, -surrexi, -ctum, *rise up, get up*
intellego, XX
intento, -are, -avi, -atum, *hold against, point at, aim*
intentus (adj.), *directed towards, intent*
interdum (adv.), *from time to time, at intervals*
interea, XXXVI

interficio, XIX
intermisceo, -ēre, -ui, -mixtum, *mingle, mix with, mix up*
intermitto, -ere, -misi, -missum, *send among, let pass*
interpres, -etis (masc.), *interpreter*; as adj., *interpreting*
interrogo, -are, -avi, -atum, *ask, question, enquire*
intersum, -esse, -fui, *take part in, be among*
intervenio, -ire, -veni, -ventum, *come between, intervene, drop in*
intimus (adj.), *inside, inmost, intimate*
introduco, -ere, -duxi, -ductum, *bring in, introduce*
intueor, -ēri, -tuitus, *look at, gaze at, watch*
invado, -ere, -vasi, -sum, *go in, attack, invade*
invalidus (adj.), *weak, ill, invalid*
invenio, XLIX *a*
invidia, -ae (fem.), *jealousy, envy*
invito, -are, -avi, -atum, *invite*
invoco, -are, -avi, -atum, *call upon, invoke*
ipse, VI
ira, XIV *b*
irrideo, -ēre, -si, -sum, *smile, smile at, mock*
irrumpo, -ere, -rupi, -ruptum, *break in, rush in*
Isthmicus (adj.), *Isthmian, belonging to the Isthmus* (of Corinth)
ita (adv.), *so, thus*
itaque (conj.), *and so, accordingly*
iter, XIV *a*
itero, -are, -avi, -atum, *repeat, say again*
iterum, XI

jaceo, -ēre, -ui, -itum, *lie, lie down*
jacio, II
jocus, LXXIV
jucunde (adv.), *pleasantly, attractively*
Judaei, -orum (masc.), *Jews*
judicium, XXVI *a*
judico, -are, -avi, -atum, *judge*
jugulo, -are, -avi, -atum, *strangle, kill*
jugulum, -i (neut.), *throat*
jugum, XIV *a*
junior (adj.), *younger, young*
jus, -ris (neut.), *right, justice*
jussus, -us (masc.), *order, command*
juste (adv.), *justly, rightly, properly*
justus (adj.), *just, right, proper*
juventa, -ae (fem.), *youth, youngness*
juventus, -utis (fem.), *youth, youngness*

lābor, -i, lapsus, *slip, glide, fall*
laboriosus (adj.), *laborious, hard, hard-working*
lac, XXXIX *a*
Lacaena, -ae (fem.), *a Spartan woman*
Lacedaemonius (adj.), *Spartan*
lacero, -are, -avi, -atum, *tear, wound*
lacesso, -ere, -ivi, -itum, *provoke*
lacrima, XII
lacus, XVIII
laetitia, XXV
laetus (adj.), *happy, glad, pleased*
lateo, XXXIII
latrocinium, -i (neut.), *piracy, brigandage, robbery*
lătus, XXXIX *b*
lātus, XXXIV *b*
laudatio, -ionis (fem.), *praise, congratulation*
lectus, -i (masc.), *bed, couch*
legatio, -ionis (fem.), *embassy, legation*
legatus, XXII
lĕgo, XXXIV *b*
lenis, XXIV
lĕvis, XXXI
lex, XLIII
libellus, -i (masc.), *small book, note, petition*
lĭber, XXVI *b*
līber (adj.), *free*
liberi, XII
libero, -are, -avi, -atum, *free, set free, release*
libertas, -atis (fem.), *freedom, liberty*
licet, XXV
lictor, -is (masc.), *lictor* (attendant on a Roman magistrate)
lilium, -i (neut.), *lily*
limen, LVI
lingua, XXVI *a*
littera, XXI
litus, XXXIX *c*
loco, -are, -avi, -atum, *place, set, put*
longe (adv.), *far, lengthily, at length*
longitudo, -inis (fem.), *length*
loquor, IX *a*

lucrum, -i (neut.), *gain, profit*
luctuosus (adj.), *grievous, sorrowful, sad*
luctus, -us (masc.), *sorrow, grief, mourning*
ludibrium, -i (neut.), *laughing-stock, joke, sport*
ludus, XXV
lugubris (adj.), *sad, sorrowful*
lumen, LVI
lupa, -ae (fem.), *she-wolf*
lux, XVIII

machina, -ae (fem.), *machine, device, siege-engine*
maestus (adj.), *sad, sorrowful*
magistratus, -us (masc.), *magistrate, official*
magnificus (adj.), *magnificent, grand, splendid*
magnitudo, -inis (fem.), *size, extent, greatness*
magnopere, XLVI
majestas, -atis (fem.), *dignity, majesty; treason*
mando, XXXII
mane (adv.), *in the morning*
maneo, XVII
manifestus (adj.), *obvious, clear, apparent*
manus, III
Mariani, -orum (masc.), *Marians, followers of Marius*
maritimus (adj.), *of the sea, by the sea*
marmoreus (adj.), *of marble*
Martius (adj.), *of Mars; March*
matrimonium, -i (neut.), *marriage*
matrona, LIV
mature (adv.), *early, seasonably, in time*
mediterraneus (adj.), *inland*
meditor, -ari, -atus, *contemplate, consider, reflect*
membrum, XXXIX*a*
memini, LVII
mendacium, -i (neut.), *lie, falsehood, deceit*
mens, LII
mensis, XXXV
mentio, -ionis (fem.), *mention*
mereo, mereor, XLIII
meridies, -ei (masc.), *mid-day, south*
meritus (adj.), *deserving, deserved, worthy*
metuo, LXXIII
militaris (adj.), *of a soldier, military*
mille, XX
minister, -ri (masc.), *servant, attendant, minister*
ministerium, -i (neut.), *service*
minitor, -ari, -atus, *keep threatening, threaten frequently*
minuo, -ere, -ui, -utum, *lessen, diminish, make smaller*
miraculum, -i (neut.), *wonder, portent, marvel*
miror, LIV
mirus, XVI
miser, XIV*a*
mitis, XLIV
mitto, XV
modestia, -ae (fem.), *modesty, restraint*
modestus (adj.), *restrained, modest*
modus, IX*a*
mollio, -ire, -ivi, -itum, *soften, soothe, calm*
mollis, LXVI
Mŏna, -ae (fem.), *Anglesey*
mons, V
morbus, XLVI
mordeo, -ēre, momordi, morsum, *bite, nibble, chew*
morior, XVI
moror, IX*a*
mors, XIII*a*
morsus, -us (masc.), *bite, mouthful*
mos, XXVI*a*
mulceo, -ēre, -si, -sum, *soothe, pacify, quieten*
mulier, LXVII
multitudo, -inis (fem.), *crowd, number*
mundus, LXXIV
munio, XXVI*b*
murus, II
muto, XXXIV*a*

nanciscor, XXXIX*d*
nascor, LIX
nasus, -i (masc.), *nose*
natio, XLIV
-ne, particle used to introduce a question
ne...quidem, LIII
nebula, -ae (fem.), *cloud, mist*
nec (in LXIV), *not even*
necessarius (adj.), *necessary*; as noun, *kinsman, relative*
neco, XXII

neglego, -ere, -xi, -ctum, *neglect, ignore, leave undone*
negotium, LI
nemo, VI
nequaquam (adv.), *by no means, in no way*
nescio, -ire, -ivi, -itum, *not know, be ignorant*
neuter, LIII
neve (conj.), *and in order that not, nor*
nex, necis (fem.), *death*
nimius, XXVI *a*
nitidus (adj.), *bright, shining, pretty*
nix, LII
noctu (adv.), *by night*
nomen, I
nomino, -are, -avi, -atum, *name, call*
nondum, XLII
nonnulli (pron.), *some, some people*
nonnunquam, LI
noscito, -are, -avi, -atum, *recognise, perceive*
novitas, -atis (fem.), *newness, novelty, strangeness*
novus, XX
nubo, LIV
nudo, -are, -avi, -atum, *bare, denude, strip*
nudulus, dimin. of **nudus**
nudus, LII
num (interrog. particle), *whether, if*
numerus, IX *b*
nunquam, XLI *b*
nuper, XXXI
nuptiae, -arum (fem.), *marriage, wedding*
nutrio, -ire, -ivi, -itum, *nourish, feed, bring up*
nutrix, -icis (fem.), *nurse*

obarmo, -are, -avi, -atum, *arm against*
obruo, -ere, -ui, -utum, *overwhelm, overcome*
obscurus (adj.), *dark, obscure, hidden*
obsecro, -are, -avi, -atum, *beg, beseech, entreat*
obses, XLVIII
obsideo, -ēre, -sedi, -sessum, *besiege, occupy, blockade*
obsidio, -ionis (fem.), *siege, blockade*
obstinatus (adj.), *obstinate, resolved, firm*
obsto, XXXVI
obstringo, -ere, -nxi, -strictum, *tie, bind, oblige*
obstupefactus (adj.), *amazed, astounded*
obstupesco, -ere, -stupui, *be amazed, be surprised*
obviam (adv.), *in the way*; **obviam ire**, *meet*
obvolvo, -ere, -volvi, -volutum, *cover*
occĭdo, -ere, -cidi, -casum, *fall, collapse, die*
occupo, XLVIII
occurro, -ere, -curri, -cursum, *meet, run into*
octingenti (num.), *eight hundred*
octogensimus (adj.), *eightieth*
oculus, XXXIII
odi, -isse, *hate*
odium, XXIII
offero, -ferre, obtuli, -latum, *offer*
officium, XLVI
olim (adv.), *once, formerly, sometime*
oliva, -ae (fem.), *olive*
omen, -inis (neut.), *omen, portent*
omnino, XXXVII
onus, XXXIX *c*
opes, LXXIII
oportet, XXX
oppidanus (adj.), *of the town*; as noun, *townsman*
opprimo, -ere, -pressi, -pressum, *overcome, oppress, sink*
ora, LV
Ordovices, -um (masc.), *Ordovices* (a British tribe)
origo, -inis (fem.), *source, origin, beginning*
orior, V
ornamentum, -i (neut.), *adornment, ornament, decoration*
orno, -are, -avi, -atum, *adorn, decorate, beautify*
oro, X
ōs (ossis), XLIV
osculor, -ari, -atus, *kiss*
ostendo, XXXIV *b*
ostento, -are, -avi, -atum, *keep showing, show frequently*
otium, XLIV
ovum, LII

paene, XLVII
paenitentia, -ae (fem.), *repentance, sorrow, regret*

palam (adv.), *openly, obviously*
pallidulus, dimin. of **pallidus** (adj.), *pale, wan*
palus, XVIII
parco, XXVII
parcus (adj.), *sparing, spare, thin*
parens, LIV
pareo, XXVI*b*
paro, III
passus, -us (masc.), *pace, yard*
pastor, -is (masc.), *shepherd*
pateo, XIII*a*
paterfamilias (masc.), *father of a family, head of a household*
paternus (adj.), *fatherly, paternal*
patesco, -ere, patui, *be open, become open, be obvious*
patientia, -ae (fem.), *patience, suffering, endurance*
patior, XLIII
patria, VII
Patricii, -orum (masc.), *Patricians, noblemen*
pauci, XI
paulatim, XLVIII
paulisper, XXVIII
paullum, -i (neut.), *a little*; used as adv.
pavor, LIV
pectus, -oris (neut.), *heart, breast, chest*
pecunia, XXIII
pecus, XXXIX*a*
pedes, -itis (masc.), *footsoldier, infantryman, infantry*
pellis, XXXIX*a*
pello, IV
pendeo, XXIX
perago, LII
perangustus (adj.), *very narrow*
percutio, -ere, -cussi, -cussum, *strike, hit, murder*
perdo, IX*b*
pereo, -ire, -ivi, -itum, *perish, die*
periculum, XIII*b*
perlego, -ere, -legi, -lectum, *read through, read thoroughly*
permaneo, -ēre, -nsi, -nsum, *remain, endure, last*
permoveo, -ēre, -movi, -motum, *move greatly*
permultus (adj.), *very many*
perrumpo, -ere, -rupi, -ruptum, *break through, burst*
perseverantia, -ae (fem.), *endurance, determination*
persevero, -are, -avi, -atum, *persevere, endure*
perspicuus (adj.), *obvious, clear*
perterreo, -ēre, -ui, -itum, *frighten thoroughly, terrify*
perturbo, -are, -avi, -atum, *disturb, upset, confuse*
pervenio, XXXIX*c*
pes, XII
pestiferus (adj.), *pestilential, bearing disease*
pestilentia, -ae (fem.), *disease, plague, infection*
peto, I
philosophus, -i (masc.), *philosopher, sage*
pila, -ae (fem.), *ball*
pilum, XXXII
pingo, LXXII
pinguis, XLIII
piscator, -is (masc.), *fisherman*
piscis, LV
piscor, -ari, -atus, *fish*
placeo, **placet**, IX*b*
placo, XXXIX*a*
plane (adv.), *plainly, clearly*
planus (adj.), *plain, clear, level*
plaustrum, -i (neut.), *waggon, cart*
plausus, -us (masc.), *applause, clapping*
plebei, -orum (masc.), *plebeians, the poorer classes*
plebes, plebs, -is (masc.), *the plebs, the lower orders*
plenus, XXV
plerique, XXXIX*a*
plerumque (adv.), *generally, usually for the most part*
poculum, -i (neut.), *cup*
poena, XXXIV*a*
Poeni, -orum (masc.), *Carthaginians*
poeta, -ae (masc.), *poet*
pondus, XIII*b*
pono, IV
pons, VIII
pontifex, -icis (masc.), *priest*
popularis (adj.), *popular, belonging to the people*
populus, V
porta, III
porticus, -us (fem.), *porch*
porto, III
portus, -us (masc.), *harbour, haven*
posco, XXII
possideo, -ēre, -sedi, -sessum, *possess*

posterus (adj.), *next, subsequent*; pl. *future generations*
posthac (adv.), *subsequently, hereafter*
postridie (adv.), *on the next day*
postulatio, -ionis (fem.), *demand, request*
postulo, XXX
potestas, X
potius, XXXVIII
praecipito, -are, -avi, -atum, *send headlong, hurry along*
praeclarus (adj.), *distinguished, famous*
praeco, -onis (masc.), *herald*
praeda, -ae (fem.), *booty, spoil*
praedīco, -ere, -xi, -ctum, *foretell, predict, prophesy*
praedo, XXXVIII
praefigo, -ere, -xi, -xum, *fix upon, attach in front*
praemitto, -ere, -misi, -missum, *send forward, send in advance*
praemium, XXXIV *b*
praeparo, -are, -avi, -atum, *prepare, make ready*
praepono, -ere, -sui, -situm, *place in front, propose, suggest*
praesertim (adv.), *particularly, especially*
praesidium, XIX
praesto, XXXVIII
praesum, -esse, -fui, *be at the head of, be in charge of, preside*
praeter, XXXV
praetereo, -ire, -ivi, -itum, *pass by, pass, overlook*
pravus (adj.), *base, disgraceful*
precor, -ari, -atus, *pray, beg, beseech*
premo, XLV
pretium, XX
prex, XXIX
primo (adv.), *at first*
primum (adv.), *first*
princeps, XLVII
prior (adj.), *first* (of two), *former*
priscus (adj.), *old, former, of the past*
pristinus, XLI *b*
priusquam (adv.), *before*
privatus (adj.), *private*; as noun, *private citizen*
probo, XL *b*
procedo, -ere, -cessi, -cessum, *go forward, advance, proceed*
procul, XVI
procumbo, XXX
procurro, -ere, -curri, -cursum, *run forward*
prodeo, -ire, -ivi, -itum, *go forward, advance*
proditor, -is (masc.), *traitor, betrayer*
prodo, -ere, -didi, -ditum, *betray, hand over*
proelium, XLI *a*
proficiscor, XII
progredior, II
projicio, -ere, -jeci, -jectum, *throw forward, throw, hurl*
prolabor, -i, -lapsus, *slip forward, fall*
promissus (adj.), *sent forward, let grow, long, promised*
promitto, -ere, -misi, -missum, *promise, let grow*
promptus, XLIV
pronuntio, -are, -avi, -atum, *announce, tell beforehand, pronounce*
propero, XXXVIII
propitius (adj.), *favourable, auspicious*
propono, -ere, -posui, -positum, *set forward, propose, place in front*
propter, I
proripio, -ere, -ripui, -reptum, *seize, hurl*
prosequor, -i, -secutus, *follow up, attack*
prosilio, -ire, -ui, *leap forward, jump up*
prosperus (adj.), *successful, prosperous*
prosterno, -ere, -stravi, -stratum, *lay low, overcome, kill*
protendo, -ere, -di, -sum, *stretch out, reach forward*
protinus (adv.), *forthwith, immediately*
provincia, -ae (fem.), *province*
prudentia, XLVIII
publice (adv.), *publicly*
pudor, -is (masc.), *shame, modesty*
pueritia, -ae (fem.), *boyhood, childhood*
pugio, XLVII
pulchritudo, -inis (fem.), *beauty*
purgo, -are, -avi, -atum, *cleanse, purify, purge*
purus (adj.), *pure, clean, bright*
putrefactus (adj.), *decayed, putrefied*

quadraginta (num.), *forty*
quadratus (adj.), *square*
quaero, III
quaeso, *I beg you, I ask you*
quamquam, XX
quando, LXX
quare (adv.), *wherefore, for which reason*
quasi, XXXVI
quatio, -ere, -ssum, *shake*
queror, X
quia, XLIX*a*
quidem (adv.), *indeed, to be sure*
quies, -etis (fem.), *rest, sleep, peace*
quiesco, LI
quietus (adj.), *quiet, restful*
quingenti (num.), *five hundred*
Quirites, -ium (masc.), *Citizens, Fellow-Citizens*
quis (indef. pron.), *anyone*
quisquam, XIII*a*
quisque, XIV*b*
quo, XXXIX*b*
quoad, LV
quomodo (adv.), *how, in which way, in what way, as*
quoniam, XXIX
quotannis (adv.), *every year, each year*
quotidie (adv.), *every day*
quotiens (adv.), *as often (as), how often*

rado, -ere, -si, -sum, *scrape, shave*
ramus, LXXII
rapidus (adj.), *swift, rapid, blazing*
rapio, XXXII
raro (adv.), *rarely, seldom, at intervals*
ratio, XXVI*b*
ratis, LXII
rebellio, -ionis (fem.), *rebellion, revolt*
recido, -ere, -cidi, -cisum, *cut down, cut back*
recito, -are, -avi, -atum, *recite, tell*
rectus (adj.), *upright, straight, right, direct*
redemptio, -ionis (fem.), *buying back, salvation, ransom*
redeo, XIV*a*
redigo, XXIX
redormio, -ire, -ivi, -itum, *return to sleep, go back to bed*
reduco, -ere, -xi, -ctum, *lead back, reduce*
refero, -ferre, rettuli, relatum, *bring back, refer*
reficio, -ere, -feci, -fectum, *repair, mend, refresh*
regius (adj.), *royal, princely*
regno, -are, -avi, -atum, *reign, be king*
rego, LI
regredior, -i, -gressus, *return, go back, retire*
religio, -ionis (fem.), *scruple, superstition, religion*
relinquo, III
reliquiae, -arum (fem.), *remains, relics*
reliquus (adj.), *remaining, rest*
remitto, -ere, -misi, -missum, *give back, send back, put down*
removeo, -ēre, -movi, -motum, *remove*
renovo, -are, -avi, -atum, *renew, replenish, restore*
repello, XXXIX*d*
repente (adv.), *suddenly, unexpectedly*
reperio, XXXI
repeto, -ere, -ivi, -itum, *seek again, return to (a place)*
reporto, -are, -avi, -atum, *bring back*; **victoriam reportare**, *win a victory*
repugno, -are, -avi, -atum, *fight against, resist*
resisto, -ere, -stiti, *stand up against, resist*
respicio, -ere, -spexi, -spectum, *look back, look round*
respondeo, XV
responsus, -us (masc.), *answer, reply*
restituo, -ere, -ui, -utum, *restore, reestablish*
retineo, -ēre, -ui, -tentum, *keep, retain, hold on to*
revoco, -are, -avi, -atum, *recall, call back*
rideo, LXXII
rigeo, -ēre, *be stiff, be cold*
rigidus (adj.), *stiff, frozen, firm*
ripa, XXIV
rivus, -i (masc.), *brook, stream*
robur, XIII*a*
rosa, -ae (fem.), *rose*
rostrum, XXIII
ruina, -ae (fem.), *collapse, ruin*
rumor, -is (masc.), *report, tale, rumour*

rumpo, -ere, rupi, ruptum, *break*
ruo, -ere, rui, rutum, *rush, collapse*
rupes, XVI
rursus, XLIX *a*
rusticus (adj.), *of the country, rustic*

sacerdos, XXXV
sacramentum, -i (neut.), *offering, sacrament*
sacrificium, -i (neut.), *sacrifice, offering*
sacrifico, -are, -avi, -atum, *sacrifice*
saeculum, XLIX *b*
saepe, XXIX
saevus (adj.), *fierce, wild, cruel, savage*
salus, XI
salutatio, -ionis (fem.), *greeting, salutation*
saluto, -are, -avi, -atum, *greet, salute*
salvus (adj.), *safe, whole, unharmed*
sanctitas, -atis (fem.), *sacredness, holiness*
sanctus, L *b*
sanguis, XXXII
sapio, -ere, -ivi, *taste, discern, be wise*
satis, XLVIII
saucius, XLVII
saxeus (adj.), *rocky, made of stone*
saxum, XIII *b*
scelus, XXXIII
scilicet (adv.), *of course, in truth, to be sure*
scriptor, -is (masc.), *writer, author*
secedo, -ere, -cessi, -cessum, *go away, depart, march off*
secessio, -ionis (fem.), *departure, secession*
secreto (adv.), *secretly, quietly, unbeknown*
secundus (adj.), *following, second, favourable*
sedeo, XX
sedes, -is (fem.), *seat, position*
seditiosus (adj.), *mutinous, rebellious*
seduco, -ere, -xi, -ctum, *lead aside, lead astray*
semel, X
seminudus (adj.), *half-naked*
semper, LXX
senator, -is (masc.), *senator*
senatus, -us (masc.), *senate* (Roman parliament)
senectus, -utis (fem.), *old age*
senex, XXII
senior (adj.), *older, old*
sententia, L *b*
sentio, XLVI
sepelio, XLIV
septingentensimus (adj.), *seven hundredth*
septingenti (num.), *seven hundred*
sequor, VII
serenus (adj.), *calm, quiet, serene*
serius (adj.), *serious, grave*
sermo, XLIII
sĕro, XXXIX *a*
sēro (adv.), *late, too late*
serpens, -tis (fem.), *serpent, snake, dragon*
servitus, XXVII
servo, XII
severitas, -atis (fem.), *strictness, severity, harshness*
severus (adj.), *severe, harsh, strict*
sexcenti (num.), *six hundred*
signo, -are, -avi, -atum, *seal, fasten, mark*
signum, XVIII
sileo, XI
similis, XIII *a*
simulac, simulatque, XXXIV *a*
simulacrum, XXXIX *a*
singuli, XL *b*
sinister, XLI *b*
sino, -ere, sivi, situm, *allow, let*
sitis, XXXII
situs (adj.) (part. of **sino**), *placed, situated*
sobrius (adj.), *sober, calm*
societas, LIII
sol, XVIII
soleo, XXXVIII
solitudo, -inis (fem.), *loneliness, desolation*
solum (adv.), *only*
solus, IV
solvo, XXIV
somnus, XXXII
spargo, -ere, -si, -sum, *sprinkle, scatter*
Sparti, -orum (masc.), *Spartans*
spatiosus (adj.), *large, spacious, roomy*
spatium, XXXIII
spectaculum, -i (neut.), *sight, spectacle, show*
specto, XXXV
spes, XIV *a*

spina, -ae (fem.), *thorn*
spolium, XXXIV*a*
squalidus (adj.), *filthy, dirty, squalid*
statim, XLII
statua, -ae (fem.), *statue*
statuo, -ere, -ui, -utum, *set up, establish*
statura, -ae (fem.), *stature, build*
sterno, XLV
stomachus, -i (masc.), *stomach; anger, wrath*
strenuus (adj.), *active, energetic, strenuous*
strepitus, LVI
stringo, XXIX
studeo, XXVI*b*
studium, LIII
stupeo, -ēre, -ui, *be amazed, be astonished*
suadeo, XII
suavis (adj.), *charming, courteous, suave*
subflavus (adj.), *pale, fair*
subito (adv.), *suddenly, unexpectedly*
subitus, II
subjicio, -ere, -jeci, -jectum, *put under, subject, subdue*
sublatus (adj.), *removed, raised*
subterraneus (adj.), *under the ground, subterranean*
suburbanus (adj.), *near the city, suburban*
succendo, -ere, -di, -sum, *set fire to, set alight*
succido, -ere, -cidi, -cisum, *cut down, fell*
sudor, -is (masc.), *sweat, perspiration*
Sullani, -orum (masc.), *followers of Sulla*
summoveo, -ēre, -movi, -motum, *remove*
sumo, XXXIV*a*
sumptus, -us (masc.), *expense, luxury, extravagance*
superbus, XX
supero, XLVIII
superstitio, -ionis (fem.), *superstition*
supersum, -esse, -fui, *be above, survive*
supervolito, -are, -avi, -atum, *fly above, keep flying above*
supplex, -icis (masc.), *suppliant*
supplicium, XXXIV*a*
surgo, LVI
suspicio, -ionis (fem.), *suspicion*
suspicor, -ari, -atus, *suspect*
sustineo, VIII
taberna, -ae (fem.), *shop, tavern*
tabernaculum, -i (neut.), *shrine, sanctuary*
tabula, -ae (fem.), *picture, tablet, list*
talentum, -i (neut.), *talent* (of silver: £240)
talis, XVI
tango, XXX
tantum (adv.), *so much, only*
tantus, XXV
tectum, -i (neut.), *roof, house, covering*
tego, LXVI
temperatus, adj. *moderate, temperate*
tempestas, VI
tenebrae, XXXIII
tenus (prep.), *as far as, up to*
tergum, XVI
terreo, XL*b*
terror, -is (masc.), *terror, fright, panic*
testamentum, -i (neut.), *will*
testimonium, -i (neut.), *evidence*
testis, L*b*
Tiberinus (adj.), *of the Tiber, consisting of the Tiber*
titulus, -i (masc.), *name, title, signature*
toga, -ae (fem.), *toga* (Roman dress)
togatus (participial adj.), *dressed in a Roman toga*
tolero, -are, -avi, -atum, *endure, put up with, bear*
tollo, XL*b*
tormentum, -i (neut.), *torture, twisting, catapult*
torvus (adj.), *grim*
tot, LV
totiens (adv.), *so often, so many times*
trado, XIV*b*
traho, XL*a*
tranquillus (adj.), *quiet, peaceful*
transeo, -ire, -ivi, -itum, *cross over, cross*
transfigo, -ere, -fixi, -fixum, *pierce, run through, transfix*
transfuga, -ae (masc.), *deserter, runaway*
transgredior, -i, -gressus, *cross over, cross*

transilio, -ire, -ui, *jump over, leap across*
transno, -are, -avi, -atum, *swim across*
transveho, -ere, -vexi, -vectum, *carry across, transport*
tremo, XXXIII
trepidatio, -ionis (fem.), *fear, panic, trembling*
trepido, LIV
tribunus, -i (masc.), *tribune* (a Roman magistrate or officer)
tributum, -i (neut.), *tribute*
triumphalis (adj.), *triumphal*
Troia, -ae (fem.), *Troy*
trucido, XXI
truncus, -i (masc.), *trunk, stem*
trux (adj.), *fierce, rough, overbearing*
tuba, XXV
tueor, -ēri, -itus, *look at, watch over, protect*
tumultus, -us (masc.), *uproar, disturbance, civil war*
tunica, -ae (fem.), *tunic*
turba, XXXVII
turbo, -are, -avi, -atum, *upset, disturb, confuse*
turpis, XIV*b*
turris, XIX
tutus, V

ubique (adv.), *everywhere*
ulciscor, XXXVII
ullus (adj.), *any* (only after negative)
umerus, -i (masc.), *shoulder*
unde (adv.), *whence, from where*
undique (adv.), *on all sides, from all sides*
unguentum, -i (neut.), *ointment, nard*
unguo, -ere, -nxi, -nctum, *anoint*
urgeo, -ēre, -rsi, *press, urge, press upon*
usque, XXXIV*b*
uterque, V
utrum, XXXVII
uxor, XI

vado, -ere, vasi, vasum, *go*
vadum, -i (neut.), *shallow, ford*
vagor, XXXIV*a*
vagulus (dimin. adj. of **vagus**), *wandering, errant*
valens (adj.), *strong, powerful*
valetudo, -inis (fem.), *health*
validus (adj.), *strong, healthy*
vallum, IX*a*
varius, LIII
vas, -is (neut.), *vessel, pot*; in pl., *baggage*
vehemens (adj.), *violent, forceful, vehement*
vehementer, XXXI
vehiculum, -i (neut.), *vehicle, carriage*
veho, XXIV
vel (adv.), *even*; **vel...vel**, *either... or*
velut (adv. and conj.), *as if, as it were*
venatio, -ionis (fem.), *hunting, hunt, chase*
vendo, LV
venenum, -i (neut.), *poison*
veneror, -ari, -atus, *worship, venerate, revere*
venia, XLIX*b*
venio, I
venor, -ari, -atus, *hunt*
venter, -ris (masc.), *stomach*
verbero, -are, -avi, -atum, *beat, belabour*
vereor, XXI
vero (adv.), *in truth, indeed*
verto, XV
vesper, XXVI*b*
vespera, -ae (fem.), *evening*
vestibulum, -i (neut.), *porch, vestibule*
vestimentum, -i (neut.), *clothing, dress*
vestio, -ire, -ivi, -itum, *clothe, dress*
veto, XXVIII
vetus, XLV
vexo, XXIV
vicensimus (adj.), *twentieth*
vicinus, LV
victima, -ae (fem.), *victim, sacrificial offering*
vicus, -i (masc.), *village, district, canton*
vigilo, XXXVI
vilis (adj.), *cheap, vile*
villa, -ae (fem.), *farm, farm-house, country-house*
vincio, XIV*b*
vinco, XVII
viola, -ae (fem.), *violet*
violo, -are, -avi, -atum, *spoil, lay waste, break (faith)*

virga, -ae (fem.), *rod, stick, staff*
viridans (adj.), *green, flourishing*
virilis (adj.), *of a man, manly, strong*
virtus, XI
vito, XLIII avoid, escape
vivus, XLV
vocifero, -are, -avi, -atum, *shout, echo, vociferate*
voluptas, XLVIII
vox, XVIII
vulgus, LIII
vulnero, -are, -avi, -atum, *wound*
vulnus, XXXVII
vultur, -is (masc.), *vulture*
vultus, -us (masc.), *face, features, countenance*

Zămensis (adj.), *of Zama, at Zama*

CAMBRIDGE: PRINTED BY W. LEWIS, M.A., AT THE UNIVERSITY PRESS